Darkness Over the Valley

Darkness Over the Valley

Wendelgard von Staden

TRANSLATED BY
MOLLIE COMERFORD PETERS

NEW HAVEN AND NEW YORK · TICKNOR & FIELDS · 1981

Copyright © 1981 by Wendelgard von Staden
Translation copyright © 1981 by Ticknor & Fields

Design: Sally Harris / Summer Hill Books

Library of Congress Cataloging in Publication Data

Staden, Wendelgard von.
   Darkness over the valley.
   Translation of Nacht über dem Tal.
   1. Staden, Wendelgard von, 2. Germany, West—
Biography.   I. Title.
CT1098.S67A3513   943.085'092'4 [B]   80-15579
ISBN 0-89919-009-X

Printed in the United States of America

V   10   9   8   7   6   5   4   3   2   1

To My Mother

This book was published in Germany in March of 1979. It is not a novel, nor is it a story. It is an account.

I put down on paper events that had haunted me for more than thirty years. I did this for my children, not for the public. The younger generation of Germans has grown up in a world so vastly different from the one we knew that they have little understanding of the circumstances that shaped our lives.

When I was first approached about having the manuscript published, I refused. What right did I have to bother other people with my memories? In many ways they were typical of my generation, but in other ways they were not. I had, after all, witnessed things that very few others of my age had seen.

One foggy Sunday in November of 1978 I visited the place of my youth for the first time in many years. The fog was so dense that I could not see much of the landscape, the hills, the little woods, the fields — all that I loved so much. But I could make out enough of the changes that had taken place. The little village had grown into a nondescript modern community. The old square church was still there, as were most of the farms. The oak tree still stretched its branches over the wall in front of the house where we had lived. But gone were the horses and cows, the dunghills and carts. The big barns of our farm stood empty; the manor house looked dilapidated. The stable for the oxen had disappeared, as had the quarters for the farmhands. In the courtyard stood a combine and other farm machines — but there were hardly any people. I was told that the farm buildings would soon be torn down and replaced by high-rise apartments.

I walked down to the little valley. There an industrious contractor had already laid the foundations for new houses. And the old dirt road was now a wide paved street. I crossed the little creek, which still ran through the valley, and went up the hill. There I found a big new gate which led into a cemetery that had not existed before. Rows of headstones stretched along the crest of the hill — simple stones with numbers carved on them. They looked oddly lost in the fog, belonging nowhere, to no time, no place. I could make out names on a few — "Saul Silvermann, born in Radom, died here in 1945" — but on most there were only numbers. In the village, church bells started to ring, but in the cemetery the sounds were muffled by fog.

It was then that I decided to give in to the publisher's request, for otherwise who would remember why those stones were there? It did honor to the townspeople that they set up this cemetery, I thought, but most of them were young and new to the town. What did they actually know about this place?

All in all, I thought — standing there among the stones in the fog, recalling how things were so many years ago — all in all my generation did not do so badly. Those who survived the war did not do badly. We had worked to repair some of the damage done by the generation of our parents. They had taught us to do our duty, to obey orders. Our feelings had not mattered. "You are nothing; your country is everything." This had been hammered into our consciousness. Self was unimportant. It was never talked about. "Pursuit of happiness" was a phrase we encountered only after we were well into our twenties. The foundation on which we had been taught to stand crumbled right under our feet. The experience of my generation had proved it to be all wrong. When we reached adulthood we were left with little to believe in, least of all the greatness of our country. Rather, we were confronted with a sea of destruction, of terror, of millions of people murdered in our name.

But overall we did succeed in what we wanted to do. We wanted no more hate around us. We wanted to become a member of the Western family of nations. We wanted freedom, and we did embrace the democratic way of life. We wanted to travel and to study abroad, to learn about other countries, other people. Trained to work hard, we became successful. Modern technology transformed our way of life in a very short time. Our people became affluent to a hitherto unknown degree, and like a shiny layer, that affluence spread over the wounds of our past. Our experience had made us careful and circumspect in matters of foreign policy. Rebuilding the fabric of our society, however, was a different matter. We concentrated on material things; we were less sure about our system of values. We became so very busy. We did not find a way to convey to our children an understanding of a crucial time in our lives. We left them cut off, without tradition, in a vacuum of history. We did this because we were afraid we would be misinterpreted and misunderstood in what we could tell them about ourselves.

And so this little book came to be published. During the many years I spent abroad, I learned that it is difficult to explain the German past to foreigners. It is my hope that this account, which I have tried to record as truthfully as memory permitted, may be a small contribution.

Bonn, May 1980   W.S.

Darkness Over the Valley

$\mathcal{A}$t that time our village, like most of the surrounding villages, was still a sleepy little country place nestled between orchards and fields. The old half-timbered houses of its farmsteads, with their steep stone steps and sagging woodsheds, huddled around the old church like chicks around a mother hen. Along the southern horizon rose a chain of softly undulating hills. Vineyards crept up their slopes to the forest, which in turn covered each hilltop like a cap.

On Sundays in the summertime, long before the war, my father sometimes walked across the main railroad tracks to the old vineyard, sat down under a tree at the edge of the forest, and painted the landscape: far to the east, the open countryside of the *Weitfeld* ("far field") with its various small tenant plots and a few large fields, which were part of our estate; to the south, the flat ridge of the Vaihingen Hills, up to which ran field paths; somewhat closer to the village, where the *Weitfeld* began, the nursery greenhouse, which was protected by a fir hedge; to the southwest, lining the road to Vaihingen, a row of tall pear trees whose fruit could not be eaten but was picked to make cider; and directly to the west, the grove of the small quarry, behind which could be seen the tower of Vaihingen Castle in the distance.

Father carefully painted in the gables and corners of our village: Farmer Wenz's house, where the tracks of the local train crossed the road from Ensingen; next to that, the house belonging to old Schank, a railroad employee; then, in the middle of the village, on the corner where the road to Vaihingen crossed the village street, the inn zur Krone; on the other side of the crossing, next to Trostel's house, the cottage of old Mathilde, who was said to be a witch and capable of killing a cow with her evil eye or healing wounds with dog's hair when the moon was full; next to Mathilde's farther up the village street, the bakehouse, where Fred, the baker, made salt pretzels every Saturday; the shop of the old Burgers, whose brothers and sisters had long since emigrated to America; the town hall and the village school; Vollmer's house and the houses of the elder and younger Bausches; Farmer Zeh's house, with the dunghill out in front on the road; and finally, part way along the road leading to the main railway station, the new white cottage of Schauer, the shoemaker.

On the other side of the village street, opposite the entrance to our estate, was the blacksmith's shop. On any day the smith could be seen bent over his hearth, pumping the bellows until the iron glowed red-hot, then hammering it into shape on the anvil. On the far side of our barn were steep steps, partly washed out by rain, leading up to the church, with its broad, square tower and a golden cock atop the high, pitched roof. Behind the church stood our estate. Set in a square around the courtyard were the spacious manor house with a giant oak tree out front, the caretaker's house, the horse stable and hay barn, the stable for oxen, the granaries, the farmhands' quarters, the cow and pig pens, and the cart shed. Under an old lilac bush in the center of the courtyard were bolted trapdoors covering the steps to the potato cellars. Above the rooftops could be seen the orchard and the trees of the park, which extended as far as the grounds of the reservoir. The reservoir itself was set on a small hilltop so densely covered with thickets that all we could see of it was the rusty tin flag of the water gauge floating in the middle of the tank. Above this scene — from the *Weitfeld* to the castle tower at Vaihingen — father painted the blue summer sky with its small, fluffy white clouds.

There had never been much to report about our village. In early times the Celts had settlements in the area. The Roman legions had left behind the foundations of a bathhouse (there had been a lake at one time which stretched from our village to the hills). Once during the plowing of a field, a lot of small horseshoes were found, which came from the horses of the Huns who'd ridden up from Lake Constance.

At school we read in the town chronicle that our village had been founded by monks from the Maulbronn Monastery, which at one time owned a great deal of the surrounding countryside. On the landmarks the bishop's crosier, which had been chiseled into the ancient, grey sandstone centuries ago, could still be seen. The monastery was a proud structure that had survived the ravages of time. Situated at the west end of the hills, it had been built by Roman monks, who had brought agriculture and the cultivation of grapes to the area along with Christianity. There was a path following the forested crest of the hills on which one could walk all the way to the monastery and there sit in the cloister watching the water running down into the fountain. Or one could follow the long, stone walkways to the monastery church, which had stood empty since the time of the Reformation. All that remained of its furnishings were a heavy wooden cross hanging over the altar, and the choir stalls. One of the brothers had carved scenes on the stalls showing how the monks fished and tilled, sowed and harvested, gathered the grapes and took them to the press. Although these choir stalls were hundreds of years old, the daily life depicted there was the same as that of the people in our village when I was growing up. On the far wall of the monastery garden there was a tower where the alchemist, Doctor Faustus, had lived. In the floor of the topmost room was a circular hole with charred edges through which the devil was said to have taken Doctor Faustus to hell.

According to the chronicle, the first settlement was established out in the *Weitfeld* at the village well. But almost everyone, even the pastor, died when the plague swept through Europe in about A.D. 1400. The nine survivors moved a little closer to the shore of the lake and built new houses. Gradually the lake dried up and became a marshy meadow. In the summertime a pair of storks, who nested on the church roof, came to look for frogs there. My father told us one could see marsh gases flickering like tiny bluish flames in the meadows at night. The farmers used to say, "the elves are dancing." My parents eventually drained the marsh and converted its rich, dark soil into fields. This made the farmers unhappy. The marsh had been there as long as anyone could remember, and they suspected that my mother, who was always one for newfangled ideas and changing tradition, was behind it. After that the storks never again came to nest on the church roof.

Our estate was also mentioned in the chronicle. In the beginning it had been part of the monastery holdings. Then it passed through the hands of several different owners until my great-grandfather bought it when he was called to serve at the court of the king of Württemberg. Actually, the house was only the family's summer residence; the rest of the year they lived in Stuttgart like other court nobility. But for the sons of my great-grandfather, the estate became a permanent home. My father also grew up there. He often walked through the fields to the forest on the other side of the railroad tracks to lie in wait for deer or wild boars until the mist began to rise in the meadows and the first lights were turned on in the village. When he walked down the village street in his loden jacket, dog on leash and shotgun over his shoulder, he would pause to greet

2

*F*ather was a tall, slender man with dark hair and an aquiline nose. He loved the woods and hunting. From the time he was a child, he had wanted to be a forester, but his parents wouldn't let him. Like most younger sons of the gentry, he was expected to become an army officer. For a few years he served in a regiment garrisoned in Stuttgart, but then army life began to bore him — so he told us — and around the turn of the century he borrowed some money and emigrated to Argentina. There he worked on ranches, eventually earning enough money to buy his own land and cattle. But he couldn't shake his homesickness, and so in July of 1914 he returned to his homeland. A few weeks later war broke out and father rejoined his regiment. He spent many months on the western front, lying in the trenches along the Somme. When the war ended and he was discharged from the army, he was unable to find work. The money he had made in Argentina vanished in the terrible inflation following the war.

My father owned only a share of the estate, as he had inherited it with his two brothers. His eldest brother had gone to the university and had become a diplomat, while the second brother had remained an officer in the German army. Thus when my father took over the estate, not only did he lack the money needed to buy up the leases of the tenants who had for many decades farmed the estate lands but he also became indebted to his brothers. When my parents married in 1922, their very survival hung in the balance. Together they worked the few fields that were not under lease. They set apart one field on the edge of the *Weitfeld* for a nursery and built a greenhouse there. Even though she had small children at home, for many years mother drove to the market in Stuttgart at four in the morning to sell the vegetables she and father had produced.

As children, we weren't much aware of the economic hardships at home, although the story was often told that a plate, which had broken at the hospital when my brother was born in 1923, would have cost 23 million marks to replace. And so many beggars came by the house — ten, sometimes twenty a day — to ask for soup and bread. They wore old army coats and shoes that had holes in them. We knew that they slept in our field barn on the bales of straw that had been stored there after threshing. We also used to find ashes from their fires while playing in the caves of the small quarry. The chalky sandstone there had once been used for houses in the vicinity, but later people began using the large quarry closer to Vaihingen, and the slopes of the small quarry were reforested. This forest and the little valley bordering it belonged to my father. He enjoyed puttering around in the woods, planting small fir trees and painting them with tar to keep the deer from browsing on them.

Despite the hard work, life in our family was cheerful. In the evenings father would play his guitar and sing songs. On the strap of his guitar mother had embroidered the motto "Per aspera ad astra," which means that one has to go through hard times to arrive at a better life. Later I often thought how this hope never became a reality for my parents.

As soon as school was out, we used to play with our friends from the village. On Saturday evenings, after the women had swept the curbstones and carried their full baking tins to Fred, the baker, we would sit on the steps inside the warm bakehouse and watch Fred retrieving pretzels and tins from the brick oven with his long wooden paddle. There, on the steps of the bakehouse, we would make plans to meet our friends.

We were a great gang in the village: Wilhelm Gutjahr, Albert Zeh, the Linkenheils boys and Else Seizinger, Günther Güller, Herta Wirth, Herbert Öhler, and Ruth Dillman. We went with them to the park where my great-grandfather had planted exotic trees. We would run past the big oak we loved to climb, down the paths bordered by overgrown jasmine bushes to an old swimming pool, which had not held water for a long time and was full of molding leaves fallen from the surrounding chestnut trees. Then we'd run through the gully, which was filled with overgrown Scotch broom and wild roses, to the beehives under the two old lindens, and out to the big pines by the Silla Hopp, a small knoll with an elm tree growing on it. There the park ended, divided from the grounds of the reservoir by a hedge. A wooden gate led out to the field path, which ran alongside the hedge. But the Silla Hopp was the place we fought for. It was stormed by white men under the leadership of Old Shatterhand and defended bravely by the Indian chief Winnetou.* In the evenings before harvesttime, when the wheat was still green on the stalk, the smell of jasmine would fill the whole park and the tops of the pines stood like black towers against a sky brightened by the moon rising over the Vaihingen Hills.

If there were lots of children to play with and we felt brave, we would scout as far as the valley and the grove of trees in the small quarry. The grass that grew in the valley was not sweet enough to be used for hay because, wedged in between a heavily forested slope on one side and a steep cliff on the other, it was rarely reached by sunlight. Through the valley meandered a brook with moss-covered banks which one could cross by a small footbridge. The pump house was there too — a dark, damp, empty brick building. Beyond it stretched the Vaihingen meadows as far west as the Enz Valley.

Old Shatterhand and Winnetou: Characters from a series of books written by German author Karl May and read by generations of German children. Set in frontier America, these novels have as their heroes Old Shatterhand, a white plainsman and Indian killer, and Winnetou, a Sioux Indian chief.

We often went down to the village railway station with our friends and sat on the bench to await the arrival of the train, which came once a day. Frau Seizinger, the station mistress, would put on her red cap and blow her whistle to signal to the locomotive, with its two little cars, that it could be on its way again. This small line, which ran by our village on its way between Vaihingen and the main railway station, was built because the people of Vaihingen were afraid of the big black "devil train," as they called it. When the line from Bruchsal to Stuttgart was still in the planning stages, around 1870, the people wanted the tracks laid at the foot of the hills, as far away from the town as possible. Later, after they had grown used to the idea, they needed a way to get from Vaihingen to the main station and had this branch line laid.

When the harvest came, there was no more time to play. Everybody in the village had to pitch in. We worked in the fields from early morning until late evening. At noon and again at four, the bells in the church tower rang across the field and we could sit down in the grass to eat a piece of bread and drink the pale cider, which tasted as sour as vinegar.

Mother used to tell us what a happy childhood we had, though the times themselves were anything but happy.

3

*W*e seldom had visitors. Those who came were mostly neighbors, arriving either on horseback or driving rickety automobiles. Carl, Eva, and Bärbl, our friends from far away, came only once for a few days before they moved from their house on Lake Constance to Berlin.

The biggest event was when our cousin Stephan came to visit. He was six or seven years older than we. He had a shock of blond hair and a wide, funny mouth, with corners which turned up in a friendly grin. He usually came with a group of friends who wore lederhosen and green shirts and called themselves the Heinrich von Plauen Squad, after the knight of the Teutonic Order of Marienburg. They belonged to the Bündische Jugend ("Youth League") founded by Admiral von Trotha. The boys all came from Potsdam as most of their fathers had been officers in the Germany army.

In the evening, after eating bowls of the goulash and noodles my mother had cooked for them, the boys would

make a campfire on the stone path, sit beside it on the
grass, and sing while Stephan played his guitar:

> Our dear lady of the fountain cool,
> Give us poor soldiers
> The sun's renewal
> Lest we die of the cold.
> With the booming, booming
> Of the drums, drums, drums,
> Hei ridi-ridi-rum,
> Onward the valiant soldier comes.

Later, they took blankets and went out to the field barn
to sleep. But once there, they'd stay awake, sitting together and reading aloud from books they had brought
in their knapsacks: a book about Heinrich von Plauen
and Marienburg, stories by Ernst Jünger, and Rilke's
"Cornet." My brother and I listened with admiration as
they spoke of their ideals and of the manly virtues they
believed in: "Let man be noble, caring, and good. . . ."

Because Stephan and his friends had made such an
impression on me, and because I, too, wanted to belong
to a group that sang songs and went on hikes, I became
determined to join the Hitler Youth as soon as a group
was formed in our village. For then, when Hitler came
to power in 1933, the entire Reich was being organized,
right down to the last village.

Old Schank's son was made the local party leader. He
had wanted very much to go to high school and then
study at the university, but his parents could not afford
it. He was talented and personable and generally liked

in the village, but he'd been without a job for a long time before enthusiastically joining the movement.

Fräulein Ilg, who lived in a room of the Maile's small shop in the upper lane — a competitor of the Burgers' shop on the main road — became the leader of the Nazi Women's Corps. Fräulein Ilg worked as a secretary in a factory in the city. She had short, black hair, which she combed severely back, and she spoke with a deep voice, caused, it was said, by smoking cigarettes — the only woman in the entire district to do so. All the women over twenty were supposed to join the Nazi Women's Corps, which met once a week to knit and sew clothing for families with lots of children and to make door-to-door collections for the Winter Relief Organization. The main reason for getting together, however, was to be able to chat and to sing.

All the boys and girls in the village had to join the Hitler Youth, and because our house had some empty rooms, one of them was used for the headquarters. Meetings were held every Saturday evening. Younger boys between the ages of ten and fourteen belonged to the Jungvolk; the girls of this age to the Jungmädchen. Young people between fourteen and eighteen joined the League of German Girls (Bund Deutsche Mädchen or BDM) and the Hitler Youth. The first leader of our Hitler Youth was Reinhold Kühner, the son of Farmer Kühner, whose small farm stood at the end of the upper lane where it turned into the village road and led out to the main railway station.

On the wall of this room, mother had painted, in

white gothic letters on a blue background, a verse that always struck us as rather odd:

> Work, not doubt and discord,
> The right of life bestows.
> New castle walls and battlements
> From a new generation grow.

It was under this inscription that the Hitler Youth gathered each Saturday. Although I was still too young to be a member, I always attended when the group of Jungmädchen had its meetings. Afterwards we practiced drills. We had to stand in a straight line according to height and practice "right face" and "left face" while keeping our hands stiff at our sides. We had to try to march exactly in time. Our squad sewed a pennant out of red cloth with a swastika in the middle and white curlicues all around. We tied it to a pole and carried it proudly through the village. Walking three abreast, we sang so loudly we became hoarse:

And whenever we march, there lights up a light
That penetrates darkness and puts clouds to flight.

So that the beat could really be heard, we stamped our right feet down so hard that they ached. Our first squad leader was Alwine Schneider, who was learning to be a seamstress in the city. Later, when she no longer wanted to do it, I became Jungmädchen leader for a time.

We young people wore our uniforms on all special occasions celebrated by the village. The boys wore black shorts and brown shirts with shoulder straps and belts, while the girls' uniform was a blue skirt with a white blouse and a brown jacket, made of fake velvet, called a "climbing vest." On May Day we all gathered on the playing field next to the train station where the Maypole had been put up. Long colored ribbons hung down from its wreath, beneath which the girls of the BDM danced the roundelay. The older people waltzed to the accompaniment of Emil Linkenheils's accordian on the cement floor of the empty barn. Afterwards they went to drink beer at zur Krone.

On Harvest Day, a Sunday in October, Fräulein Ilg and the members of the Nazi Women's Corps decorated the church altar with ears of corn, sheaves of wheat, cabbages, apples, and brightly colored Michaelmas daisies from the gardens. When the church service was over, everyone went home to eat onion tarts and drink new cider that had been fermenting in jugs.

Our old church was small and plain and could barely hold all the people of the village. The bell rope, which was pulled by a boy after the sermon every Sunday, dangled down next to the altar. On the wall by the pulpit hung an enormous picture of Jesus in white robes with head somewhat inclined and arms outstretched, walking on the water.

Every year in November, the village celebrated Remembrance Day to honor those who died in the First World War. The bells rang early in the morning, and the whole community gathered for the church service. After church everybody went down the narrow steps to the war memorial that stood below the church near the road. My father, being the head of the Veterans Association, placed a wreath at the foot of the monument and said a few words about a soldier's love for his fatherland. In the front row around the monument stood the members of the Hitler Youth. Behind them were the men of the village, wearing their best black suits and holding top hats in their hands; then in black coats and scarves were the women, among them the war widows. Of the fewer than five hundred people in our village, twenty-four men had been killed in the First World War. Their names were chiseled on the stone. After father's speech, "The Song of the Good Comrade" was sung:

> I had a loyal comrade,
> You'll never find a better,
> Always side by side
> Into the bitter fight
> We marched along together.

We had to sing another sad song, about Flanders, because it was one of my father's favorites:

> In Flanders field
> My life lay sealed
> In a coffin in a shroud.

> Who lies within,
> I cradled him,
> I nestled him, a boy so proud.

At this point during rehearsals, the girls of the BDM began to giggle, making Reinhold, who was coaching us, furious. "This song is about a *mother*," he admonished. When the final verses came, Emma Linkenheils began pulling on the rope in the church, so that the heavy bells would toll above our heads, signaling the end of the ceremony:

> When peace bells ring
> Their sounds will bring
> Joy to many and more.
>
> But I must wander
> To that field in Flanders,
> Alone to ponder
> The grave of the babe I bore.

We would have preferred to sing another song that Reinhold had taught us, but father wouldn't permit it. The Hitler Youth all over Germany knew it:

> On a coal black steed comes Death astride,
> Wearing a hood, his mien to hide.
> When soldiers march into the fray,
> He and his courser gallop their way.
>
> Death can also pound the drum.
> Your heart can feel its rolling hum.
> Loud and long he makes a din
> Beating on a dead man's skin.
>
> As he beat the first drumroll
> The spark of life drained from the soul,
> And as the second roll was played
> The soldier in the tomb was laid.

> The third drumroll will not be over
> Until God's grace has touched the soldier,
> The third drumroll is soft and deep
> Like a mother rocking her child to sleep.

Many who sang these songs with us then, later lost their lives. Young Schank was killed at the very beginning of the war. Günther Güller and the Linkenheils boys never returned, nor did Wilhelm Gutjahr. Reinhold Kühner was listed as missing on the eastern front. I cannot remember whether the church bells were rung at the end of our war. I don't believe they were. But as we sang about the black hood of Death and mothers visiting their sons' graves, we had no idea what lay ahead of us.

It was with a mixture of envy and admiration that we watched the Ensingen Jungvolk as they marched one day along the road toward Vaihingen. They were a larger group and even had drums, trooper's drums that were painted with a black-and-white pattern and hung down from their belts all the way to their ankles. They marched along arrogantly, three abreast, past the inn zur Krone and Farmer Gutjahr's house, looking neither right nor left. Their song resounded joyously off the walls of the houses:

> The wind is blowing with a sting
> Around the rain-soaked tents.
> Geldern is falling to the king,
> His horsemen storm the battlements.

We had no drums like those of the Ensingen group and certainly couldn't march as well, but we made campfires on summer evenings and sat around dreaming of the peasant wars and armies of knights which our songs told us about:

> The peasants wanted to be free
> And that was hard to do.
> But pour a glass of wine for me
> I'll sing the song for you.

Or we felt like poor, scorned, defiant gypsies:

> Unruly fellows by windstorms blown,
> Princes in tattered cloth,
> We'll fall beside a grey milestone
> Dishonored even in death.
>
> . . . .
>
> But out there by the side of the road,
> There with the King of Thorns,
> The fiddles' lament sounds far and wide
> Crying to the Lord our grief.
> And the Crowned One sends down
> Comforting tears with his dew.

Or we were proud young horsemen riding along hidden pathways beneath dark pines out into the dawn:

> Hooves a-clatter on the bridge,
> Our troops on battle bent,
> A bloody fight up every ridge,
> That's why we were sent.

> We are riding and riding and riding,
> From afar the war drums beat.
> O Lord, keep us strong in the battle,
> Then our lives will be complete.

I have never been able to forget those songs. Their strong beat and somber, mystical words held us in thrall. Later, whenever I was sad or afraid, I would sing them to myself.

Before the outbreak of the war, Stephan and the Heinrich von Plauen Squad came by to see us one last time. They were on a hiking trip to the Carpathians. The boys no longer wore green shirts, but brown ones, and even their songs sounded different. They told us they had been forced to join the Berlin Hitler Youth. After being badly beaten up, they finally all agreed to join so they could stay together. In the evening they gathered in the yard as Stephan strummed cheerfully on his guitar:

> A soldier tall tra-la, tra-la
> With beard and all tra-la, tra-la
> What will my mother say?

Then sitting very straight and serious, he plucked at the strings:

> A little thrush sings in the East,
> A song so beautiful.
> It sings of love and kisses,
> It sings of dying, too.
> 'Twas then I thought of you.

Because Stephan and his friends were just about to take their final exam, the *Abitur*, they talked a lot about what careers they wanted to pursue. Stephan wanted to study history, "to become a professor," he said, with his nose in the air. But his friends all thought it more fitting at the time to become army officers. Mother objected vehemently. She always became vehement at such discussions, and we dreaded her reaction. "But Tante Dette," pleaded Stephan, "the German army is formidable. Even *you* have to admit that." And, indeed, she had to.

The boys said their good-byes and started toward the railway station. They went past the church and Maile's shop, where Fräulein Ilg was looking out the window. Their boots and soot-covered cooking pots dangled from their knapsacks. Stephan's guitar was flung jauntily over his shoulder. The boys' clear voices rang out over our garden:

> Wild geese fly the northbound route.
> Their cries pierce nighttime's hush.
> Unsteady flight, watch out, watch out!
> What has become of us?

From the curve by Farmer Kühner's house, where the lane turned into the village road, the wind picked up their tune and carried it back to us:

> We're fighting in the kaiser's name,
> Like you an army grey.
> And if we don't come back again
> "Amen," the autumn winds will say.

4

*A*t that time my uncle, my father's brother, was our country's foreign minister, and our name was well-known throughout Germany. But a rift had developed between the brothers over the estate, and our families had little to do with each other.

Nonetheless, my uncle played an important role in the lives of us children. To a certain extent he was always present. My parents talked about the debts they still owed him, and in the village all the people were proud of him. For them, it was as though this famous son of the village had brought back the old times when the king would travel from his castle in Stuttgart in his fine horse-drawn coach to pay a visit to the master of the estate.

When my uncle's big automobile drove through the village from the cemetery where my grandparents were buried, all the villagers dropped what they were doing and ran to wave. My brother and I also raced down to the main street to see his automobile. My brother always hoped that someday it would stop and the great man would lean out the window to say, "So, my boy, how are things going?" But the big car never did stop, and my brother had to choke back his tears. For my mother's ways and the peculiar views she held had only served to deepen the rift between the families.

All this did not affect me much. My only wish was to get home from school as quickly as possible so I could help hitch up the horses and drive out to the *Weitfeld*, where the breezes bent the stalks of wheat and the fields of rape blossomed into gold. But later, when we were older, we were sometimes invited to tea at my uncle's estate, where he lived when he was not in Berlin. His fields bordered ours up on the Vaihingen Hills. Thrilled by such an invitation, we would climb onto our bicycles and ride along the field paths, where the wheels of the farmers' carts had left deep ruts, up over the hills and down to my uncle's villa, which stood in a small park surrounded by large trees.

Whenever my uncle was visiting his estate, he did what my father did: donning loden jacket and leather breeches, he would go into the fields with his gun slung over his shoulder to hunt for partridges or hares. On his birthday, singing clubs and youth groups from the surrounding villages came out early in the morning to serenade him. He was so well liked by everyone that people thought as long as he was in the government things couldn't really go wrong. Only mother criticized him, and she did so to our consternation. "He only raises false hopes," she would say."He couldn't really stop a thing."

It must have been 1937 when I saw the Führer myself. He was to deliver one of his famous speeches in the town hall in Stuttgart, the very spot where mother had heard him speak six years earlier. My parents had obtained tickets for this rally and promised to take us. I was overjoyed. Then, unexpectedly, father refused to go. He said he hated this kind of thing with all the shouting and carrying-on. He complained that we Germans had become a nation of boors — impudent, tactless, and terribly arrogant. But in the end he agreed to accompany us and, with a wry expression on his face, pinned on the party badge. (A year before, the local council had decided to join the party, and my father had always been a council member.)

We drove on narrow roads through the villages, arriving at a large parking area in front of the Stuttgart town hall. It was almost nightfall. Storm troopers were directing traffic with flashlights. Thousands of people thronged the entrances. Hitler Youth units marched past us with banners, while military music blared from loudspeakers and floodlights beamed into the sky.

Once inside, I stood behind a barricade near the center aisle of the hall. Dignitaries of the state and party were already gathering in front of us on a specially erected stage. Beneath this stage stood various groups with trumpets and flags. Excitement swept through the hall. Waves of jubilant cries could be heard outside rolling closer and closer. Now the trumpets proclaimed, "Youth, youth, knows no fear. . . ." The tumult outside was growing to a storm. The guards took up their positions inside and stood at attention. A hush came over the crowd. The "Badenweiler March" was played, commands rang out, spotlights danced brightly on the ceiling. I managed to push my head past the arm of the storm trooper in front of me and could see the aisle leading back to the entrance. A group of men was approaching; a couple of steps ahead of it — the Führer. Thunderous cries of "Heil! Heil!" greeted him right and left as row after row of people raised their arms in the Nazi salute. Suddenly he was right in front of me. There were his brown shirt and shoulder straps, his hand raised in salute, his dark hair falling across his forehead. He stared straight ahead, past the crowd. It seemed as though he saw no one. His eyes were very blue. I wanted to scream, but I could not. I was struck dumb. I saw him slowly striding in high boots. I saw his eyes, so blue they seemed fluorescent. Then he was past me. As he mounted the stage and stood at the rostrum, the hall became absolutely still. Then, to the accompaniment of the trumpets, thousands sang "Deutschland über Alles" and "Raise High the Flag," while the storm troopers lining the center aisle stood at attention.

As our automobile pulled into the courtyard late that night, I still could not bring myself to speak. I did not want to hear what my mother was saying. My feelings had been stirred. I swore deep in my heart that I would die for the Führer if that was what he wanted. And I dreamed of that man with the slow stride, his eyes directed at something far away which no one else could see.

Somewhat later that same year, the first mobilization took place in our area. In the middle of the night the village suddenly came alive. Motorcycles roared down the street. We heard unfamiliar voices shouting orders. Jeeps drove into the courtyard and officers wearing long coats got out. A whole staff was quartered in our home and in the caretaker's house. Young men in civilian clothes came from all over, carrying small suitcases. Taciturn, stiff, and awkward, they had just received induction orders. With flashlights beaming this way and that, the men were divided into groups and driven off in trucks.

Later that night, Farmer Gutjahr came to see my father in the living room. He kept running his cap through his hands as he spoke dejectedly: "I wanted to ask you, do you think there's gonna be war now? My boys, they're of age. I just can't handle the farm all by myself."

Father calmed him down. "Take it easy. It's only a drill. There isn't going to be any war. They'd be foolish to do that; it would be the end of everything." Gutjahr took my father's hand in his own work-worn, peasant ones and thanked him.

But the war came anyway. Farmer Gutjahr's son Wilhelm, a pale, hardworking boy with whom we had often played in the park, was called up. So was his brother Emil. And Wilhelm never came back. For many years the old farmer had to work the farm alone, with only the help of his wife and his daughter.

5

I've dared all things with forethought
And none would I gainsay,
But may they come to naught
If myself I did betray.

One day I shall carve these lines by Ulrich von Hutten* on a wooden plaque and fasten it to the wall of the village cemetery beside my mother's grave. She had long predicted what was to come and year after year she had had to watch it unfold, right up to the bitter end.

She was a peculiar and passionate person, my mother. She never lacked for opinions on the political scene. Though this merely embarrassed us children, it often made father downright angry. Whenever he got fed up with hearing mother's political views, he'd say, "I'm getting on my horse now and riding away from here,"

Ulrich von Hutten: Knight and poet, born in 1488. Leader in the peasant wars against the Duke of Württemberg.

and he would go into the quarry grove to plant fir saplings.

Mother grew up in a castle on the Rhine which her father had bought as a ruin and restored. It must have been rough going for that little girl's French tutor, who often scolded her, saying, "You are as stubborn as an Irish dog." When mother was fourteen, she wanted nothing more to do with tutors, nor did she want to go to school in the city. What she did want to do was to learn farming and work with the horses in the fields. Her parents let her have her way, and she enrolled as an apprentice on a nearby farm. When the First World War broke out and German farm workers were drafted into the army and replaced by prisoners of war, my mother was called home to look after her parents' fields.

While high-ranking German officers billeted at the castle sat in the Knight's Hall discussing the situation on the western front, mother was out with the prisoners of war harvesting the wheat or picking cherries in the orchard. She took the corn to the mill by way of a steep hill path, and at night she'd haggle over coal and seed with the skippers of the boats in the harbor.

Among the prisoners who had been assigned to their farm was a tall, dark-haired Russian, who gave nightly speeches in the prisoners' barracks. Because he spoke German well, he attracted not just his fellow prisoners but people from the neighborhood as well. Every night more of them came to listen — Germans who no longer believed in victory, who simply had had enough and wanted an end to the monarchy and above all to the war. Hunger and cold had become facts of life at home, while at the front the men kept right on dying. Rumors about conditions on the western front spread up and down the Rhine more quickly than elsewhere in Germany. Mother frequently eavesdropped through the thin barracks walls as the Russian spoke of the bolshevik revolution, of overthrowing the government and fundamentally changing society, of the solidarity of the working class. She overheard his audiences end their meetings with the "Internationale," which extolled the rights of the people. On such nights she became witness to a world her parents knew nothing about. She began to cast hostile glances at the officers in the castle, who were still busy planning new offensives against the Allied armies in France.

After the Germans had lost the war, her father was forced by the French to step down as district administrator of the Rhine Province, and the castle had to be sold. Mother began to take an interest in political literature. She read Karl Marx and Lenin, examined social democratic writings, and decided finally that her own political philosophy came closest to that of the Fabians. She hoped that the socialist center would hold its own against the right and left and that the Weimar Republic would be able to cope with the country's distress. She shared with many an increasing despair over the League of Nations and the Treaty of Versailles with its harsh reparations. But, contrary to my father, she thought the Nazi rise to power was a catastrophe. She saw the pitfalls that remained hidden to so many of her compatriots.

On a winter evening in 1931 at the Stuttgart town hall, there was an assembly at which Hitler was to speak. Mother and some of the neighbors drove there to hear him, while father stayed at home with us children and painted. A fire was going in the big tile stove, for it was bitter cold outside and starting to snow hard.

Then mother came home. With coat still draped over her shoulders and heavy boots on her feet, she went over to the stove and opened the vent. The reflection from the fire cast a red glow over her. "I saw Hitler," she said, and paused. "That man is going to make it. The people — you should see them — they act like they're drunk. And when he makes it, he's going to rearm. And when he rearms, there will be war. And if there's war, then our country will be destroyed."

In her hand she had a large pencil that had been distributed at the rally, on which were printed the words of the Horst Wessel song.* In an ominous tone of voice she began to sing:

With flags held high
In close formations drilled
Storm troopers march with slow, determined stride.
Good comrades whom Communists have killed
March along with us in spirit side by side.

"We'll have to listen to that a thousand times more," she said.

---

*Horst Wessel: A young storm trooper who was murdered by the Communists in the late 1920s and became a Nazi martyr.

Father thought she was exaggerating as usual and tried to calm her down. But I have never forgotten the shadow her heavy winter coat cast against the wall in the firelight or the words she used that night.

After Hitler came to power, mother considered going abroad. Some of her friends who did not, later mysteriously vanished. But there was my father, who was twenty years her senior, and two small children, plus the house and farm. Then, too, Germany was the only country she had ever known.

Her political books were packed away in bushel baskets and taken out to the little bee house in the park, where they were hidden in the empty beehives. Later, I used to go there from time to time and read the books, mostly *Das Kapital*, for I was looking for something about Jenny von Westphalen. Mother had often spoken loyally of her and was angry that the great Marx had not taken better care of his wife, Jenny, even allowing her to give birth on the bare floor. But I found nothing in Marx's books about his wife.

The condition of women was mother's constant concern. "Women, whatever happens on earth, your fate will always be the same," she quoted sometimes. "Women have to work and bear children and have nothing to say. They are ignorant, uneducated, and unable to defend themselves. . . ." And as I looked around more closely, this did indeed seem to be true. The farm women worked from dawn to dusk. Leaning over their washtubs, they scrubbed shirts on washboards until their fingers were raw. They trudged into the fields wearing thick wool stockings over the sores on their legs, which refused to heal. During threshing, they stood all day long in the dust of the threshing machine, putting in the sheaves. Never, not even once, did these women have a day off. Oh, maybe on Sunday for a couple of hours after church, providing all the dinner dishes had been done. But then, right after that, would come the milking and the supper preparations. Once the wife of a farmhand sobbed to my mother, "If I'm pregnant again, I'll drown myself." She had six children already and the family was exceedingly poor.

Yet, eventually mother did take part in some Nazi activities. Maybe it was because she had seen so much poverty during the years of crisis that the economic revival going on in the country impressed her. Maybe it was the easing of the debt on our estate that made her feel she could no longer remain such an obvious outsider. Or perhaps it was simply her passionate nature and her curiosity about everything around her. But whatever the reason, she did begin to participate.

Much to Fräulein Ilg's delight, mother appeared at the evening meetings of the Nazi Women's Corps. She took part in courses for farm women and gave lectures to the girls of the BDM about further training and education.

But when the family sat around the living room at night listening to the news on the radio, mother would often react angrily to what she heard. "Now the conservatives think he's one of them. Now he's got them right where he wants them," she said, laughing scornfully as she looked at a photograph of Hitler in one of the illustrated magazines. He had just been elected chancelor and was shown, gloves and top hat in hand, bowing respectfully to the old Reich president Hindenburg.

Mother followed everything Hitler did with absolute fascination, almost as if she herself had some personal involvement with him. In response to all the propaganda — for a national community in which the old class distinctions would disappear, for creating new jobs, for the development of all the organizations which, one way or another, would eventually encompass almost everybody — she often commented angrily, "He's winning everyone over. He's even winning over the working class. The man's a genius."

Things got better in the village, too. In the little house at the crossroads, a washing machine was installed for everyone's use, and a milk depot was built onto the bakehouse. The milk was brought in from all the cowsheds, strained, separated, and taken back home as clean milk. The milk was also tested, and a few cows had to be slaughtered because they were carrying tuberculosis.

Throughout the country a process of debt remission for farmhouses and farmlands still carrying mortgages was instituted, and this probably saved my parents from bankruptcy.

Much to the dismay of us children, mother always hoped that the French and English would do something to stop Hitler. When the news came that our troops had occupied the Rhineland, father made everybody in the house go down into the potato cellar. Our area, he pointed out, was within range of the guns on the Maginot line, and the French would most certainly start firing. We sat hunched up next to the potatoes waiting for something to happen, but nothing ever did. Afterwards we secretly made fun of father for making us do this. Mother thought the French had made a great error since Hitler would now think he could get away with anything. Later, in 1936, all the nations of the world gathered in Berlin for the Olympics and we were exhilarated by the triumphs of the German athletes.

However, when it became clear that the war really would come, mother withdrew completely from all party activities. She tried to create for herself and the prisoners of war working on our farm and in the village a world that lay beyond the reach of national hatreds. As soon as the prisoners arrived, mother would explain to each and all — whether they were Poles, Frenchmen, or Russians — that here there would be no war, here we would all quietly work together for our daily bread. As the German army conquered country after country, from Norway to Africa, she would shake her head and say that we'd be victorious only unto death. With such extensive conquest, what plan for peace could Hitler possibly have, she wondered.

When she heard that the Russian campaign had started, mother became completely distraught. It was around noontime and Josepha had just brought the dishes and tablecloth into the room to set the table. We were standing around the radio listening to the continuous newscasts from the front when suddenly, and in great agitation, mother grabbed the tablecloth and flung it over the plates. "See how this cloth covers the plates?" she cried. "That's how the Russian snow will bury our soldiers. They'll lie under the snow on the Russian earth, shot down, frozen stiff, starved to death."

More than thirty years later, I would again be reminded of this scene. It was a November night and I was standing at the window of the Red Arrow, the train that travels in a straight line from Moscow to Leningrad. I pressed my face against the windowpane to get a better look at the landscape. There, flat as a pancake, lay the countryside covered by a thin, white layer of snow. All at once I saw them lying there: Reinhold Kühner, Karl and Eck, Stephan, and Rolf Potmann. I saw them lying on the Russian earth beneath the thin blanket of snow, which was just as white and smooth as the tablecloth mother had thrown over the plates that day.

6

Slowly and relentlessly the war approached. The tension increased from crisis to crisis, and the expectation that something irrevocable would happen hung over us like a storm cloud. Thus when the war finally did start, it brought almost a feeling of relief. Even Frau Krebs, my coworker in the onion fields, put down her pitchfork suddenly one day and surmised, "It would be better if they started the war now. It'll come anyway."

The Polish campaign was over quickly, and the first prisoners of war started arriving in our village. A group of twelve Polish soldiers came to work for us, the fear of dive-bombers still clinging to their bones. They came into the servants' quarters, ashen-faced, wearing thick coats and fur hats. The first thing we did was offer them something to eat. Then mother tried to find out if any of them could speak a little German so she could ask a few questions, but the men were so busy eating that they said nothing. When a cat meowed at the door, they recoiled, for the sound reminded them of the howling Stukas. A few of these first Polish prisoners of war remained with us for the duration: Josef, a waiter from Warsaw; Szigmund, a farmer; and Franzishek, who said proudly that he'd served with the Polish cavalry.

Everyone in the village who was at all fit for military service was being drafted. Fields once leased out were offered back to my parents to farm because, with so many sons away, the older men simply couldn't handle the work alone. At this time most of our own land was still under lease to a sugar factory, so these fields became like a new farm for us. There were some small buildings on the southern end of the courtyard which we turned into stables and barns. With horse and cart, cows and pigs, and the nursery and its greenhouse, our little farm began to take shape. It was mother who looked after it all because father had been drafted into the District Army Command.

There were also trainloads of female forced laborers from Poland who came to work on the farms. That's how we got Josepha. She was a small, pudgy, good-natured woman who reigned in our kitchen. Jadga, who was not quite fourteen, came too. She had had typhus and had lost all her hair.

Of all our workers, Szigmund was the one mother liked best. He was a fair-haired, stocky man, smart and industrious. He was put in charge of the others and allowed to drive the tractor, which he did with great pride. Mother told him again and again that he should

learn whatever there was to learn on our farm so that
he could use it on his own farm in Poland after the
war. One by one, the relatives of our Poles arrived too
— that was possible if you knew how to get along with
the officials. Szigmund's brother Jan came from Poland,
and Felix, Franz's brother, was sent to us from a prison
camp. At Josef's request, mother managed to get his
wife, Michalina, out of occupied Warsaw. Michalina was
very frail and coughed incessantly. It turned out that
she had tuberculosis and had to be placed in the hospital. But after a while the authorities sent her back to
Warsaw, where she soon died. Josef mourned a long
time before consoling himself with dark-haired Maruscha from the Ukraine.

With the Polish campaign over so quickly and German
troops now occupying France as well, the terrible fear
of war that had gripped the village lessened somewhat.
Yet the moment the Russian campaign began, all that
changed. This time mother was not the only one who
expressed fears: my father also talked a lot about Na-
poleon's armies and how they became bogged down in
the Russian winter.

On the same day mother threw the tablecloth over
the dishes, I had gone to the inn early in the morning
to buy sausage. The butcher, a tall, lanky man, was
standing behind the counter in his white apron slicing
sausages when the news came over the radio from a
small loudspeaker hanging on the wall behind him: "At
3:15 this morning our troops crossed the Russian border."

The butcher laid down his knife and listened. Then

slowly and deliberately he trimmed the sausage, saying as he did so, "Now it's going to get nasty. Now we're really in for it." And that was the feeling everyone had.

Quite a few men from our village had already been killed in action. And now many of the troops were being transferred to the eastern front. Soon we heard that hundreds of thousands of Russians had been taken prisoner, so many that they could not be transported and were starving to death in large numbers.

Then came the first Russian winter. Rumors circulated that our soldiers had not been properly outfitted, that they were freezing in their thin military coats and that their boots were stiff with ice. A few came home on leave limping; their toes had become frostbitten and had been amputated.

Our family doctor, Dr. Wetzel, had also been drafted. One time when he was home on leave and had come to see my mother, I happened to be in the room as he was about to leave. At the door he hesitated, took my mother by the arm, and said he had something to show her. He fumbled in his uniform pocket and took out a packet of photographs wrapped in paper. "You won't believe me," he said wearily. "I can't believe myself what I've seen in the Ukraine. Nor will I ever forget it."

He held out the pictures for mother to look at, pictures of men and women loaded on carts. Pictures of a huge trench filled with human beings lying heaped up, one on top of another. Dead. Men, women, children.

"Jews," said Dr. Wetzel. "Behind the lines they're purging the villages of Jews. They're driving them into the woods and killing them, and the Ukrainians are helping them do it. And," he added, his hand still clutching my mother's arm, "we soldiers can't do a thing. If anyone knew I had taken these photographs, my life would be in danger. Tell me, are we supposed to fight a war for *this* kind of thing?" Then, straightening his cap, he departed. A few days later he was back in his field hospital on the eastern front, working day and night with his amputation saw.

Following that first Russian winter, trainloads of forced workers were sent from the occupied Russian territories. Whoever needed workers — and that was everyone, farmers and businessmen, craftsmen and factory owners alike — could go to the railway station and collect them as the trains came in. Since we had more and more vegetable fields under cultivation and could not possibly get the work done by ourselves, we went with Szigmund on the tractor to the Stuttgart station.

Trains from the East were rolling into the huge concourse. It was evening. Guards were standing on the platform. With white billows of steam, large locomotives still crusted with snow came puffing to a halt on the tracks. Out of the boxcars poured hundreds of women. "A slave market," muttered my mother. Holding themselves erect, the women cautiously stepped down from the cars; they wore long skirts and heavy padded jackets over loose blouses. Bundles were balanced on their heads.

The guards allotted us ten workers, all young girls. We learned from their documents that they came from

a village in the Ukraine called Vilika Vovnianka. We
settled the girls in the house by the nursery. They had
a large room with beds and washbasins on one side and
benches and tables where they could eat on the other.
At first mother worried about them because of the great
numbers of Polish and Russian male workers in the area.
But the girls did not let anyone near them, at least not
until Josef was admitted after Michalina's death. The
girls from Vilika Vovnianka stayed with us until the end
of the war.

7

*A*fter grammar school my brother and I were sent to high school in Ludwigsburg. The school had formerly been a boys' high school, and there were still very few girls attending classes there. In 1942, a year before their scheduled graduation, the boys sat for exams and received emergency diplomas because they'd all been drafted into the army.

My brother tried to sign up too. Although he was two years older than I, we were in the same class because he was a diabetic. It had been hard on him having to give himself insulin shots twice a day and now the pharmacies were running out of the drug. All his schoolmates had registered for military service and every boy in the village was going off to war, but the army wouldn't accept my brother. Since he didn't want to be left behind, he joined the Northern Volunteer Legion of the Waffen-SS, a unit specially formed for the war against Russia. This unit was composed of volunteers from Switzerland, Holland, and Finland. My brother was assigned to work for a Swiss doctor in a field hospital as a motorcycle dispatch rider. He would also be able to get insulin there. Before leaving for the front, he paid us a last visit. None of us thought we'd ever see him again.

I dreamed of my brother repeatedly. There he would be in his uniform with his forage cap on, walking slowly along a path through the fog. I wanted to cry out and grab him, but he would just keep on walking without looking back until he was swallowed up in the fog.

I was sent to Berlin to study for my final exams and stayed with a friend of my parents. Uncle Fridl, as we called him, lived very quietly in a large house in Dahlem. Fate had treated him badly. First his wife had deserted him and gone to Switzerland, leaving him to care for three children. His only son, Carl, had later been killed in the war. Eva, his second child, had been drafted into the Women's Labor Corps, so only Bärbl, the youngest, was still at home.

In 1939, a few months before the war, we had gone to visit Uncle Fridl in Berlin. Mother thought we ought to get to know "the only really big city in Germany." I remember Carl then as a handsome youngster with thick, black hair and large, dark eyes. He had wanted to be a painter. During that visit, he took me to an exhibition of paintings that had officially been banned as decadent. The pictures hung above a bookstore in a loft to which Carl had access. At first I was shocked by them. They looked distorted to me; I could not figure out what they were supposed to represent. But Carl explained them to me and even gave me a small painting by Franz Marc — *Red Horses in a Yellow Meadow* — when he saw that I liked it.

Uncle Fridl worried a lot about his son because Carl often went out in the evenings with a group of friends and refused to say where they were going. Carl told me that if forbidden to go, he would simply pretend to be taking a bath, then leave the water running and climb out the window.

During this visit, Carl also showed me a painting that he had done. He called it *City in Turmoil.*

"Good Lord, Carl, are you frightened?" I asked him, because the picture showed green houses with crooked walls, a violet sky, pipes dangling from ripped-open walls, a sagging bathtub on a second floor, and people in the streets with blank disks in place of faces.

"Sure, I'm frightened," Carl replied, and slid the painting back under his bed.

One night the door to the library was ajar and I overheard a heated conversation between Carl and his father. "You can't do that," Uncle Fridl shouted angrily. "You simply can't do that." He called my father in to offer his advice.

"Ernstl," he said, "the boy wants to *desert*. My father was a soldier. I was an artillery officer in the last war. Our family has always served the fatherland faithfully. Now *this*."

Carl argued back that he was totally opposed both to what Hitler stood for and to the war. He wanted to go to Switzerland, where his mother was, and paint.

Both fathers tried to reason with Carl. Nobody wanted the war, they said, but the fatherland had to be defended. Fear had to be overcome. Running away simply was not done. Besides, Switzerland was not such a safe haven either. Sooner or later it might happen that Switzerland would also have to be occupied.

As I listened, I really didn't know what to think; though actually, I also believed that it was cowardly to desert.

In the end Carl stayed. He was drafted and soon became an officer. He marched into Russia with his regiment, and they got as far as Mount Elbrus when he was shot in the spine. For several weeks he lay paralyzed and then he died. He was supposed to have kept a diary, but I never got to read it.

Carl had already been killed by the time I went to school in Berlin. I had to study very hard to keep up with my classmates because they were much further along in their studies than we had been at Ludwigsburg. The girls were also quite different from girls I had known before. For instance, when the Schiller memorial was melted down for its metal, the girls in the class wrote a poem, which they hung on the empty pedestal that night. The following morning many people crowded around it until someone came and took the piece of paper away. The poem had been circulated in the classroom, however, and we knew it by heart:

You finally managed to destroy him,
Him whose spirit nourished our spirits well.

A new Gessler hat is hoisted in Berlin,
But only wait, there'll come a Wilhelm Tell.

and it ended:

Oh, woe to the folk who their allegiance swore
To little men like Spiegelberg and Wurm and Moor.

And everybody knew who was meant by that.*

Later when Bärbl and I were helping to extinguish
fires during one of the first air raids on Berlin, Carl's
painting suddenly sprang to life before my eyes: houses
whose walls no longer stood upright, whose fronts were
torn away; a crumpled, green bathtub and a few tiles
still clinging to the wall; pipes dangling out into space;
the strangely colored sky; and it seemed that the faces
of the people running around trying to extinguish the
fires had no features.

The news of Stephan's death reached us around the
time of this air raid. "He gave his life for the German
Reich," the notification read. After his exams Stephan
had become an officer like his father. During the war
he'd come to visit us several times. He came right after
the Polish campaign and was extremely depressed all
through his stay because his best friend had been killed
in the Tucheler Heide. They sent his friend's body home
and it was laid to rest beside the Castle of Solitude,
which overlooks Stuttgart. In the morning Stephan went

*Spiegelberg and Wurm and Moor: Villains from Schiller's plays *Kabale und Liebe* and *Die Räuber*. In the girls' poem, these names are allusions to Göring, Goebbels, and Hitler, respectively.

up there and sat beside the grave in the sunshine. When
he returned in the evening, he said nothing. Cradling
his blond head in her arms, mother wept.

Another time he visited us from France. "You weren't
able to do it, Uncle Ernst," he said to father proudly,
"but we were. We've beaten the French. The Somme
wasn't so difficult, but crossing the Aisne, now *that* was
really tough."

Stephan had come back from France in very good
spirits and he spoke glowingly of French women. In the
evening we walked to the upper gate of the park behind
the Silla Hopp. The wind carried the smell of wheat up
to us from the fields below, and a sliver of moon hung
in the sky. "On your wedding day," he said to me, "my
friends and I are going to hang the whole park full of
lanterns. Then we'll all dance with you and you'll be
wearing your long, white dress."

He came for the last time right at the beginning of
the Eastern campaign. His brow bore deep furrows and
the corners of his mouth no longer turned up in a grin.
He seemed to have aged. "You can't imagine how tough
these Russians are," he told mother. "I had to search
a captured commissar. His coat was draped over his
shoulders and he was leaning against a tree, smoking
a cigarette. When I pulled back his coat, I was aghast.
His whole side was missing! But there he stood, upright
against a tree, smoking."

Stephan thought that we would defeat the Russians
somehow, but that it was not going to be an easy campaign. He became a first lieutenant in the Regiment

Grossdeutschland. After having been grazed by a bullet, he was taken to a field hospital. Hearing that one of his men lay wounded between the lines, he had his driver take him back to the front so he could rescue the man. That's when it happened. Both of his legs were shot off and he bled to death.

After Stephan died, Rolf Potmann was the only member of the Heinrich von Plauen Squad still alive. Rolf was a Stuka pilot. When he came to Berlin on leave, he telephoned me in a despondent mood. I went to visit him at his mother's small apartment. She was a war widow — her husband having been killed in the First World War. "I don't want to be the only one of our group left," he confided to me. "I don't want to survive this thing completely alone." Whatever I said to try to console him fell on deaf ears. Several weeks later his plane was shot down.

Shortly before we were to take our final exams, our class learned that we, the entire graduating class of the girl's school, were to be sent east for war duty. We had talked a lot among ourselves about what it was really like on the eastern front. Most of us had some idea because our fathers or brothers were there. I didn't want to go, and for some reason my name was not on the list of those called up for service. So, diploma in hand, I packed my suitcases, boarded a crowded train out of the Reich capital, and returned home.

8

*I*n the meantime, my parents had moved from the big house into the caretaker's house. The upkeep of so many rooms had proved too expensive and they weren't all needed, so the house had been rented to the Women's Labor Corps.

Every morning the labor corps members stood around the flagpole next to the lilac bush in the center of the courtyard and sang songs while the flag was being raised. Afterwards they went to help out on farms and to assist women with large families.

In order to avoid doing official service, I went to an agricultural training farm near Heilbronn. Since I wanted to study agriculture, I would have had to do some practical training anyway.

However, this apprenticeship was not an easy one. At 4:30 in the morning the bells would ring for the first time. I'd drag myself out of bed, wash quickly with cold water, and pull on my work pants and boots — heavy army boots just like those the soldiers wore. Then I would run downstairs to see the foreman, who'd tell me what to do to get ready for the work scheduled that day: sharpen hoes on the big whetstone, repair baskets in the barn, count sacks, and so forth.

Between 6:30 and 7:00 we would have breakfast with the foreman and the girls who worked in the farmhands' kitchen. The bells would ring again at 7:00, and the manager, standing on the steps of the house, would assign jobs to all the workers.

The manager was a tall, lean, dark-haired man in his early fifties. He had a small walrus mustache and was reserved and forbidding. As a Mennonite, he was known for being an excellent farmer. There were no other Germans to do the field work except myself, the foreman, and the manager's younger brother — both men having been declared unfit for military service. The others at the training farm, about eighty in all, were prisoners of war or forced laborers from Poland, Russia, and the Ukraine.

During those first weeks it rained steadily. The Russian girls and I had to hoe nettles from the field path. I quickly developed blisters on my hands, and on my feet as well because the big boots never completely dried out and my socks stuck to my heels. I was able to learn some Russian from the girls. Every day they walked to the fields barefoot, carrying themselves proudly in their long skirts and singing melancholy songs as they went. When the rain finally let up, we started hoeing peas. The tiny plants grew in rows that seemed endless. Hour after hour we would whack through the rain-hardened earth with our hoes. In the mornings frost still lay on the fields and our hands were cold. Then the sun rose higher, and by noon the sweat was pouring off our faces. A lunch of bread and cider was brought out to us, and by the time evening came, we walked home exhausted. For supper we always had cottage cheese and fried potatoes; only on Sundays was a piece of sausage added.

After the peas had been hoed, the work began to get better. I had to run the machine that sowed the wheat, and once the sugar beets had sprouted, the manager put me in charge of the team of oxen which day after day pulled the cultivator through the fields. I had to be very careful to see that the animals didn't trample the tiny plants, so I wound the reins tightly around the muzzle of the lead ox and guided him between the furrows by pushing with my shoulder.

On this training farm there were many different kinds of vegetables under cultivation, vegetables we had to plant on rainy days. There were pole beans and tomatoes, cucumbers and cabbages. In June, when the peas ripened, hundreds of women and children pickers came from the city. They were brought to the pea fields each morning in trailers pulled by a tractor. I was in charge of weighing the sacks of peas. I sat at a folding table near the scales and recorded the weight of each sack in its pickers' notebook. At night I drove the last cart full of peas back to the farmhouse. For weeks on end I weighed peas.

Our work was interrupted by constant air raids because the fields were adjacent to an airport where some night fighters were stationed. One day I was standing up in the cart, driving it to the fields. The oxen, which the Poles had trained to be driven with a lead rope, were lumbering along. The cart made such a racket that I couldn't hear anything. When I got to the fields, there wasn't anyone to be seen. I pulled the oxen to a stop and looked around. Then I heard the manager calling from under a tree in an angry voice, "If you don't care about your own life, must you get the oxen killed as well?" The planes were directly above me. I dove off the cart and ran to a ditch.

I got on very well with one of the Poles, a man named Wendri. He was supposed to have worked with a circus before the war, and all of us, even the manager, handled him with kid gloves because we knew he always had a knife at the ready. I kept him informed of the news I heard on the radio and he, in turn, taught me that you don't have to do everything the hard way. "Better lazy than stupid," he said as he took the heavy crossbar from my hand and hung it on the horse's collar.

Wendri couldn't stand the Russians. Sometimes he looked at me out of the corner of his grey eyes and said cautiously, "Hitler good, yes? Poland kaputt. Germany kaputt. Russia, no, no kaputt," and then he would break into a stream of Polish.

The manager also had lots of sugar beets under cultivation, vast fields of them stretching row after row to the horizon. When the time came for them to be thinned, everyone at the farm pitched in. The hardiest plants had to be held back with a small short-handled hoe while the thickly clustered weaker plants were plucked out by hand. We worked our way through each field in a wide row. If one of us got too far ahead of the others, Wendri would give a whistle to signal that person to slow down. In the mornings we worked the rows in a stooped position, but by afternoon we were inching forward on our knees. Whenever someone straightened up in the field, the manager would be there with his dog in an instant yelling, "Hey you, get to work! Don't just stand there rolling the spit around in your mouth till it freezes." I came to loathe the very sight of sugar beets. My knees grew black right through my work pants, and every night my back ached.

We were thinning sugar beets when the *Rotschwänzchen* ("Red Tails") strafed the field. These were small French fighter planes, so called because their tails bore the bright tricolor emblem. They flew in very close to the ground from over a slight rise in the field. That day, with the sky a deep blue and the sun tinged with gold, it was impossible to think of anything bad happening. I didn't see the planes coming until I heard Wendri's voice. Then the earth started spattering up around me in little mounds. In a flash everyone else disappeared into the ditches, but before I knew what was really happening, the *Rotschwänzchen* were already gone. At the airport behind us several German planes could be seen going up in flames.

I had been working on the farm for quite a while and

could think of little besides not oversleeping in the morning, trying to eat enough bread and jam during our brief breakfast, always remembering to lock the barn door at night, and how pleased the manager would be if I could cure the oxen's infected hooves with compresses.

I needed all my wits about me during the cucumber picking, which I had to supervise. Since gherkins fetched a better price than mature cucumbers, the manager got very angry if too many of the green gherkins were left hanging hidden from view on green stems under green leaves. We worked all day Saturday and until lunch on Sunday, during which time I thought of nothing but the task at hand.

Then one day a letter from a soldier arrived for me via army mail. Although the writer of the letter said he had met me once at school, I couldn't remember him at all. He was now stationed at an army post and asked me to send him a photograph. He apologized for writing but said that he'd become an officer cadet and would soon be sent to the front, where every soldier needed to have a girl back home he could think about.

I had some difficulty answering this letter but did so and included a photograph. After that, letters began arriving regularly. I learned that he was nineteen years old, in the armored infantry, and that he had been put in charge of a platoon. After a time his letters started coming from the eastern front. Then one Sunday afternoon he appeared at the door. He was slender, with a delicate face and dark blond hair. He took off his officer's cap and bowed. Both of us felt very self-conscious and we decided to go for a walk. He began to talk about Russia. He didn't say anything about the war but spoke of the little Ukrainian villages with their broad, muddy roads, and of nights when the soldiers lay under the trees and someone played softly on the ocarina while nightingales sang in the underbrush and the steppe spread out in the moonlight. The men would sit around thinking of their girls back home and they would sing a song about a soldier keeping a lonely watch for the fatherland on the banks of the Volga. When I walked with him to the station, he bowed low and kissed my hand. Then he told me, almost apologetically, that the life expectancy of a lieutenant at the front was now twenty-three days. His letters still came for a few months; then they stopped. I don't know what happened to him, but he never returned.

In July 1944, I was cutting wheat with the tractor and binder. All day long, from morning after the sun had dried up the dew until evening when it sank beneath the horizon, I sat on the tractor alone, laying row after row of sheaves in the field. As the wind drifted over the broad, lonely fields, I thought about the lieutenant and about Stephan, who was dead, and I sang against the roar of the tractor.

After one of these long workdays, I drove back to the farmhouse and saw everyone standing around in the courtyard. The girls, the Russians, and the Poles were all clustered around Wendri. A group of farmers from the neighborhood, who had come to pick up straw, were also there. "Have you heard?" the manager shouted to me. "Somebody tried to assassinate the Führer."

"What!" I answered. "Is he dead?" In one instant the whole world had shifted.

"No," yelled the manager. "The Führer is alive," and something in his voice warned me not to say another word. Wendri's eyes were opened wide and his face was twisted in a grimace. The girls wept, but the farmers cursed. Their sons were fighting at the front, assailed from every side by the enemy, and yet the very same officers who had ordered their sons to the front in the first place had now tried to kill the Führer. The farmers couldn't understand it. "Treason," they said, "high treason."

Not long afterwards, mother came to get me. "You have to come home," she said. "Even if the plan for the assassination had succeeded, it would have come too late unless the Western powers had made peace immediately."

The Americans had already landed in Normandy and were advancing through France.

9

When I returned home at the end of July 1944, much had changed. My parents looked thin and careworn. The Polish workers had been away for months erecting fortifications in France and had only just returned. There was a new man living at our farm, an Alsatian. He didn't look well and had been thrown out of Alsace with his family for some unknown reason. Josef's son was crawling about the place, and a child of Szigmund's lay in the crib while Nina sang Ukrainian lullabies. All the horses had been confiscated by the army, except for one and it was lame. Fuel for the farm machinery was almost impossible to get — though one could obtain small amounts on the black market in exchange for butter or meat. But the unauthorized butchering of animals carried a jail sentence, so it had to be done after dark and all traces washed away before daybreak.

Mother's face had grown angular and severe. She went around in a long jacket the village tailor had made for her from khaki-colored cloth. It looked like part of a uniform from some foreign army. She got furious whenever father mentioned that we might still win the war because of a miracle weapon being developed. If we didn't make peace with the West *immediately*, she insisted, all would be lost. In the evenings she went outside and circled the house to make sure no one was there. Then she drew all the shutters, turned on the radio, and listened to the "International Report" from Switzerland by I. R. von Salis. It was as if von Salis's even, matter-of-fact voice and Swiss accent had a calming effect on her. She never missed his broadcast, not even for a single night.

The air attacks had grown fierce. On many days, especially when the weather was clear and bright, a distant humming would begin around noon. We'd stand in the yard and peer into the skies. Then they would appear: two, three, ten small silver airplanes, high, high above us. The distant hum turned into an ominous droning as thirty, forty and more planes gathered in the blue sky. It was eerie, like a force of nature. Then the countless tiny silver planes would suddenly go into formation and fly off in some predetermined direction. As they did so, the droning sound waned and finally stopped altogether. Then the special reports would come over the radio. They had bombed Ludwigshafen. Mannheim. Schweinfurt. Würzburg.

In the evenings people congregated at the milk depot. Old mother Schneider brought milk out of the barn on a cart, while Frau Seizinger distributed butter in exchange for coupons and pushed the empty milk cans on for rinsing.

Nightly blackouts were being strictly enforced. If there was a sliver of light showing anywhere, someone would immediately come to report it.

Life in the village had changed in still another respect. After sunset strangers came into the village and attempted to barter for food: onions and lard in exchange for nails and wire. It was said they came from an OT (Organisation TODT) camp. The OT had been set up to build weapons factories behind the lines, to erect fortifications, and to lay roads. These people were not Germans but foreigners of all different kinds. There were entire gypsy families, men with black mustaches and women wearing long, multicolored skirts. Frenchmen and Hungarians, Estonians and Letts all made their way through the village. And the number of those who knocked on doors at night increased steadily. When mother learned that they came from a camp that was being built in the Vaihingen meadows below the pump house, she took me with her to have a look at it.

We went down the path to the quarry grove, behind which stretched the meadows. At the edge of the forest we ran into a barbed-wire fence patrolled by guards. Mother talked with the guards for a while and they let her through, but they wouldn't let me go with her. Although it was getting quite dark, I had played there so often as a child that I knew every tree and shrub. I crawled alongside the barbed wire under the fir trees and up a small slope. Pulling aside some loose slabs of stone, I wiggled under the barbed wire on my stomach. Then I made my way to the path that led into the camp.

Down below, an entire city had sprung up. Wooden barracks covered the meadows as far as the eye could see. People scurried about talking in foreign languages. There were little children crying and men standing around in groups or hunched down in the doorways. I could see a fire burning in a wood stove and could smell soup cooking. Someone was playing a harmonica. A woman emptied a basin of dirty water right at my feet.

I saw mother standing with a group of men who were telling her in broken German that they were Hungarians and had recently been transported there to construct the barracks. They said they were from the OT and were helping to build a big underground factory in the large quarry near Vaihingen. They had very little to eat, which was why they were stealing anything they could lay their hands on in the supply barracks to trade with the villagers for food. They were free to leave the camp in the evenings after their work was done, but the authorities didn't want Germans from the surrounding villages coming in — and I don't believe that any, apart from mother and myself, ever tried to.

We left by way of the little wooden bridge that crossed the creek. There, right next to the bridge, lay rolls of barbed wire and wood for still more barracks. The Hungarians had said a special camp was to be built on that particular spot. While mother went through the gate,

I crept under the barbed wire again, shoved the stone slabs back into place, and ran after her. She took me by the arm, shook her head, and said, "The whole of Europe — subjugated by us — there in the Vaihingen meadows."

On a grey, rainy day a few days later, I went with my parents to the large quarry, the "construction site," as it would be called from then on. We walked along the railroad tracks and up the slope, from which we could see into the quarry pit.

It lay sixty or more meters deep between steep rock walls. On the side near the river valley was a broad, as yet unquarried hill of limestone, which dropped off almost vertically.

The countryside was so changed as to be unrecognizable. Barracks stood everywhere in the fields that bordered the construction site. Flat grading wagons, pulled by small, shaggy Russian horses, moved over the muddy roads. There were mountains of cement sacks and piles of iron girders and wire coils. Farther away, in the fields surrounding the quarry, stood huge cement mixers.

We were stopped by an officer who asked us to identify ourselves. When he found out who my parents were, he offered to show us around the site. From the rim of the quarry we were able to see directly into the vast, almost circular pit. Ladders had been fastened to the stone walls and men were climbing down them with heavy sacks slung over their shoulders. The whole floor of the quarry was covered with square iron pilings, which were sunk in even rows and jutted up like rusty fingers pointing skyward. On the wire fence a plaque with the name of the company that for many years had worked this quarry — Baresel and Sons — swung in the wind.

"A factory will be built here," explained the officer. "It'll be several stories high. The iron pilings are for cement pillars, which will support the ceilings of various workshops. The whole thing will be covered with semi-circular slabs of concrete, making it completely bomb-proof. These cement slabs will be cast in the fields beside the quarry and then moved to the site on tracks."

Then the officer added in a low voice that the following was for my father's ears only. In this factory a new kind of aircraft would be built. These planes would take off from shafts which they planned to cut into the face of the cliff and would fly straight out into the river valley. Thus an open runway would no longer be needed; the runway would be hidden inside the shaft. He stressed the utmost importance of this project to the Reich.

"You see?" said father on the way home. "The miracle weapon is being built after all!"

Mother was shocked. "Yes," she replied, "and right on top of us. The construction site will be reduced to rubble before it's half finished! What a devilish business. . . ."

10

*A*nd that is exactly what the construction site became: the devil's business. The *Rotschwänzchen* attacked constantly. Several times a day they flew over the site, shooting at anything that moved. Antiaircraft guns were mounted everywhere and shell fragments from defensive fire flew as far as our house. Orders were given for the construction of Tobruk shelters in the village. These were cylindrical holes in the ground just big enough for one person to stand in. They were dug everywhere: around the edge of the village, in the woods, and in the nursery. Each had a lid made out of two boards with a handle attached underneath. Cinders were stuffed between the boards to absorb the impact of flak. Whenever the sirens on the railway station wailed, those working anywhere near the construction site ran as quickly as possible to one of these shelters.

It was autumn and everyone was busy with the harvest. The threshing machine in the field barn was kept running until late at night. The straw bales that the machine produced were stacked up in the barn. In the old vineyard the early apples were ripe, and in the *Weitfeld* the tractor pulled the stubble plow over the harvested fields in preparation for seeding. Next to the cold frames in the nursery, a large field of bush beans was ripening.

Josepha had supper ready by the time we came back from the fields in the evening. "Come please. Supper ready!" she would call out.

One day two SS officers drove up to the house and asked to speak to my father. They were shown into the living room and conferred with him there in private. After they had gone, father was deeply distressed. He told us they were expropriating the valley for military purposes. The entrance to the valley would be blocked and no one would be allowed to go in. However, father had pleaded with the officers to let him and the members of his family have access to the woods of the quarry, and they had agreed to make an exception for us.

From the woods we were able to observe barracks being built in the valley; they were similar to those already erected in the pump house meadow. We could watch as trucks came over the hills from the other side and building materials were unloaded. High barbed-wire fences and watchtowers were erected in the fields around the meadow. "That's the special camp," commented mother, "and it has nothing to do with military purposes."

We watched as transports of prisoners in grey striped uniforms arrived. The watchtowers were manned. Day after day heavily guarded prisoners tramped over to the construction site to work there.

Barracks for the guards were built outside the fences, around the brick pump house. "Those people in the camp are criminals," said my father. "It's a good thing they're so well guarded." The grove and the little valley, which we had loved, became strange and sinister to us.

One day an order came from the rationing office in the district seat saying that our farm was to deliver straw and food, particularly beans, to the camp. My mother announced to the officials that before the beans could be delivered they would have to be picked and at the moment we didn't have time to pick them. If the rationing office wanted beans, then they'd better send someone over.

Josepha had just finished making breakfast. I'd returned from the barn, where I had helped with the milking and feeding. We sat down to eat around the old, square table. Then we heard it: a strange shuffling sound coming from outside the house. It sounded as though something heavy was being dragged rhythmically over the ground. Mother went to the window and, leaning out with both hands on the sill, peered into the courtyard. Then she exclaimed quietly, "What in God's name is that?" I joined her at the window and looked out toward the lilac bushes, behind which stood the flagpole, its flag raised. What I saw was a procession of thin, staggering figures with shaved heads and greenish faces. They shuffled along in wooden clogs, their jackets and pants hanging loosely. SS guards wearing grey army uniforms, with chin straps unfastened and machine guns over their shoulders, walked alongside.

They stopped in front of our house, and one of the guards came up to the door. He announced that this was the work detachment from Camp Wiesengrund which was here to get the straw and beans. It was the first time we'd ever heard of Camp Wiesengrund. What they were referring to was our little valley. "What sort of prisoners can these men be?" asked my mother. "They look like they've just stepped out of a madhouse." The guard explained to her that they were Jews and that they had come to collect the food.

Felix and I were told to hitch up a cart and go with some of them to the field barn to load bales of straw. The prisoners walked behind the cart, but we had to stop every so often because they simply couldn't keep up with us. The guards cursed, but that didn't make the prisoners move any faster. When we finally got to the field barn, we pulled the cart up to it and I told the men they could start loading the bales. These straw bales were rather heavy, being about one meter long, pressed compactly, and held together with wire. The prisoners tried to climb up the high stacks and carry down the bales, but instead they would slip, and slide down the pile themselves.

The guards began beating the prisoners, yet these men uttered no sound. Out of breath, their eyes cavernous and faces pale green, they continued to struggle with the bales. It was obvious that they couldn't manage them. Felix swore and started to load the bales himself.

Plucking them up by the wire, he tossed them effortlessly onto the cart while I stood by and watched. A sudden fear came over me, and I told the guards that they should stop and go back to the house, that we'd bring in the straw ourselves. Then I turned around and ran home.

When I got there, the other prisoners were crouching by the lilac bushes. It had rained the day before, so the ground was muddy and sodden. Mother stood next to a large kettle of potatoes cooking over an open fire. Steam was billowing out from under the lid. "These people are starving," she said. "First they've got to have something to eat."

When the potatoes were done, two Russian girls removed the kettle from the fire and poured out the steaming water, which flowed over the muddy ground. With the shuffling sound made by their wooden clogs, the detachment from the field barn now returned. Mother raised the lid of the kettle and announced that the potatoes were ready. Then something unexpected happened. They all rushed at the kettle, knocking it over and causing the hot potatoes to roll out onto the ground. The men grabbed at the potatoes, fought over them, began to bite into them; then, using both hands, they stuffed them into their mouths — boiling hot and dirty as the potatoes were. They gobbled them down and, crawling on the soft, wet ground, tried to grab for more. There was a tumult around the upturned kettle as they fought over every single potato. The guards cursed and started striking the men with their rifle butts. "What

kind of people are these, anyway?" mother asked, horror-
struck. "They're no longer human beings."

"They are Jews," replied the guard, "subhumans. You
can see that for yourself."

I was standing next to mother, when suddenly we
heard a man's voice behind us. The voice itself was low
and soft, speaking in good, clear German, but there was
an undertone of almost menacing fury. "It's *you* who've
made us into animals, and you'll pay for what you've
done to us."

We turned around and looked into a pale, emaciated
face, into immense grey eyes cast over with a sickly
haze. A round prisoner's cap was perched balloonlike
on top of his clean-shaven head. He was a young man
and the only one who had not fought for the potatoes.
He stood somewhat to the side, observing the struggle
with fists clenched.

For a moment mother was silent; then, making an
effort to keep her voice under control, she said to the
guard, "There will be no beatings here. Stop what you're
doing. I don't want to have anything to do with you.
Now leave!" She turned away, calling back over her
shoulder, "I'll send the stuff to the camp." Then she
took me with her into the house.

Breakfast still sat untouched on the table. Again we
heard the shuffling noise, until it slowly subsided.

Father had been watching everything from the window. None of us felt like eating anymore. Mother paced
back and forth in the room, her hands plunged deeply
into the pockets of her jacket. "Do you realize what it

is, that so-called *special* camp?" She turned to my father. "It's a concentration camp, it can *only* be a concentration camp. And do you know what that means? If the front comes any closer, they'll kill those people — that is, if they haven't already died of starvation by then. And what a clever spot they've chosen! In the valley of all places, so hidden away no one could ever find it."

"Keep out of this," my father said almost threateningly. "It has nothing to do with us. We can't do a thing about it." And then he grabbed his walking stick and went outside.

Mother continued to pace, talking as if to herself, "Those people are simply starving. That's it. They're half-crazed with hunger. Where do they come from? That man was right, we've made them into beasts, into subhumans. *We.*"

Only one thought flashed through my mind. We had to do something, and fast. I'd go to my uncle and ask him for help. He would do something. To be sure he had retired to his estate some time ago and no longer played an active role in the government, but he was still well known and would be able to make his influence felt.

I got on my bicycle and rode out along the upper lane, past the milk depot to the nursery. I turned onto the path going through the *Weitfeld.* The sun was shining and there were people out tending their crops.

I passed carts slowly being pulled to the fields by cows. Beside the carts walked women with babushkas tied round their heads and rakes over their shoulders.

The villa door was ajar when I arrived, so I dropped my bicycle down in the grass and ran into the house. My uncle came out of a room to meet me. He was wearing his loden jacket, and the two spaniels with him yapped their welcome. "Well, well," he said in a friendly manner. "And what brings *you* here?"

"I've got to talk to you," I exclaimed. The sunlight flickered through the blinds. I noticed a large, red geranium standing on a windowsill inside the room. I told my uncle what had happened that morning at our house and how my mother thought the camp was a concentration camp. They were Jews, I said, crazy with hunger and so weak they couldn't even lift a bale of straw. "Please, you've got to help."

My uncle drew himself up and looked down at me. I saw something in his face harden. "Don't bother me," he said harshly. "Don't bother me with this business!" Then he turned on his heel and went back into the room where the red geranium bloomed. The two spaniels followed him.

On the way back home my bicycle jounced in and out of the ruts in the field path. A summer breeze floated across the *Weitfeld*, but I did not notice it — for the air seemed heavy with the sound of wooden clogs dragging over the earth.

I saw my uncle only once more, shortly before his death almost twelve years later. He'd returned home after a long and bitter imprisonment. It took me many years to understand the look that came over his face that day when I asked him for help. It had been despair — despair mixed with fear — rising briefly and then immediately suppressed again because he knew that he could do nothing, absolutely nothing. But I didn't perceive it at the time.

11

*T*here was a small room in our house which mother used as an office. It was there that she worked on the bills and taxes and paid out wages. Her desk was constantly overflowing with papers. One Sunday early in September of 1944, she cut a poem out of the newspaper and hung it on her office door:

> September
> Once again so many colors
> For a parting
> Which pains you deeply.
>
> The last light —
> Embittered by the poison of things to come.

It turned out to be a golden autumn. Dahlias and asters were blooming in the flower garden, the hollyhocks planted along the wall swayed in the breeze, and out in the apple orchard golden pearmains and juicy russets were already ripe. Cider apples and pears were gathered up from under the trees and taken to be fermented.

By the dim light of a stable lantern, Szigmund worked away at the cider press in the machinery shed. After dumping the apples into the press, he would walk in a circle around it, pushing the rod. The juice ran out into a tub, which Franz in turn carried on his back down to the barrels in the cellar. The dregs were thrown on the dunghill next to the ox barn. The smell of new cider mingled with that of potatoes and the damp leaves that lay under the trees in the park. The wheat in the *Weitfeld* had already been harvested. Only the beet fields, with their large, thick-leaved plants, lay as a band of green between the acres of stubble.

Hanne, our gardener, had already left by this time. On the day she arrived, Hanne had wandered into our courtyard and, approaching the house, had asked to speak to mother. A young woman, short of stature, she wore thick glasses and had her hair done up in a knot at the back of her neck. She was wearing a long, worn-looking jacket and was carrying a large bag. She asked mother for work — as a gardener, she said. The fact that she was out of work struck us as odd because gardeners were in great demand then; in fact, you couldn't get one at all. Mother conversed with her cautiously. Finally, Hanne confessed that she'd lost her last job because she was half Jewish. She told us that her father had been vice-mayor of Berlin and that she was looking for refuge.

At first, I was rather taken aback by my parents' decision to let Hanne stay with us. Jews were thought to be strange and dangerous; yet I had hardly ever met a Jew myself. Since childhood I had heard bad stories about them and knew that they were persecuted and put into camps.

Many years ago, I remembered, when driving with mother to town, we'd passed an old man with a limp pulling a small rack wagon. Sewn onto his long coat was a yellow emblem.

"What's that?" I asked.

"The Star of David," mother replied. "All Jews have to wear it. They're persecuted by Hitler because they're of a different race."

"Because they crucified Jesus," I commented. That's what our teacher had told us.

Father had a Jewish acquaintance who owned a factory and had purchased an old castle near us. One time when father came back from visiting him, I heard mother pleading loudly, "Tell him that he'd better get out of Germany. And fast!"

Father's response was that the man was a good German citizen, that he'd been decorated with the Iron Cross in the war — how could anyone have anything against him?

Much to mother's relief the man got out of the country with his family before it was too late.

When we first went to high school in Ludwigsburg, there was a slender boy in our class who was Jewish.

One day at the end of a break, a fight broke out. It had started in fun; I don't really know why. But then two boys from our class began hitting this boy and he started bleeding and fell over a bench. The English teacher, who had just entered the classroom, broke up the fight immediately and had the boy escorted home. He never returned to school. It was said that he left the country with his family. Our class was confused by this incident, and no one ever talked about it afterwards.

On the way to school, beside the railway station, there was a newspaper stand. Though mother had forbidden it, we often lingered there and looked at the issues of the *Stürmer* hanging up — at the horrible caricatures and stories about crimes Jews had supposedly committed.

One time near the railway station I saw a group of people leading two girls down the street. The girls' heads had been shaved and they were crying. There were signs hanging around their necks saying in big letters, "I slept with a Jewish pig." They were being paraded outside the station by men in uniforms, and there were people standing around jeering. I didn't tell anyone at home what I'd seen that day.

When I had an appendicitis attack and was in the hospital at Karlsruhe, a nurse came into my room one morning crying. She told me that the windows of Jewish businesses all over town had been smashed. She'd once taken care of a Jewish woman and all the members of the woman's family had been so nice and friendly to her. Now they had to suffer like this!

On the wall opposite my bed hung a portrait of the Führer which I had to look at all the time. Another girl, who had come to take my temperature, said, "Do you think the Führer knows about it? I doubt he does."

After she had gone, the nurse looked at the picture, muttering under her breath, "What a devil!" It was then that I began to wonder for the first time whether the Führer was in fact an evil man.

I also recalled the professor who visited us from a university to do research on sugar beet seeds. He wanted to cultivate a seed that would produce only one plant, so the beets would not have to be thinned out. Because this was such an important agricultural project, he stayed on to talk and eat with us. We children were there too. All at once the conversation touched on the question of race. He turned to my brother and me and said how careful one must be when distinguishing good seeds from bad, that it was exactly the same with people — the Jews were simply an inferior race, and the German people must be kept free of them. "What an ass!" father commented when the professor had gone.

During my last year of school, the history lessons had dealt almost exclusively with the Aryans. They had always been superior, we were told, way back to the Brahmans in India. We thought it was ridiculous and made jokes about it.

Thus when Hanne first came to stay with us, I was disturbed about it. Mother wanted me to get to know her and sent me to the gardener's house to see her. I went under protest, but to my surprise I discovered that

Hanne was a very nice person. We sat together on her bed talking for a long time. Her brother had been classified unfit for military service and had not been drafted. She showed me a picture of an emaciated young man standing with a shovel in his hand over a ditch — in a labor camp. Hanne also talked about her elderly parents in Berlin; she worried a lot about them because they were without means. With her hands folded in her lap, hands grown rough from gardening, she studied me thoughtfully through her thick glasses. On the few occasions when I was allowed to come home from the farm where I worked, I would go to see Hanne as soon as I arrived. That she was half Jewish never bothered me again.

Thus Hanne became our new gardener, working all day in the nursery with the Russian girls. Toward the end of June she became ill and mother got her into a hospital with the help of a friendly doctor. Sometime after the twentieth of July, the day of the assassination attempt, mother took a letter that had come for Hanne to the hospital. In the letter it said that her parents had been arrested in Berlin. Hanne wanted to leave the hospital at once to see if she could help get them free. "That'd be foolish," mother told her sadly. "Something would only happen to you, too." Mother knew that as long as Hanne stayed with us she would be safe. But Hanne did leave. We never had any word from her, and it wasn't until after the war that we saw her again and learned that she'd been arrested and put into Bergen-Belsen.

12

*W*e were still the only people in the village allowed access to the path through the small quarry. Only from there could one look down into the camp and see the barracks which stood along the winding brook and watch the prisoners walking around in striped uniforms, patrolled by armed guards. On the hill that closed off the north end of the valley there was an old clay pit. Every morning a line of people bearing stretchers made its way up the narrow path leading to the pit. The stretchers were tipped into it and a white substance scattered around. Then the procession would return to the camp. Soon a strange odor, heavy and foul, began to pervade the valley, creeping up as far as the village.

On the day the detachment of prisoners had first come to our farm, Felix took bales of straw and a couple of sacks of beans down to the camp. He told us afterwards that he'd had to unload it all outside the fence because the guards wouldn't let him go through the gate. "Jews in that camp!" said Felix, and he spat on the ground.

After that, the rationing office made no more requests of us for a while. However, what that prisoner had said by the upturned potato kettle had set my mother thinking. It was as if his words had suddenly brought home to her what was really happening to these people. And she concocted a plan to help them.

She tried to discuss it with my father once or twice, but he stated clearly that it would be impossible to do anything for them and warned her not to get involved, that it would be terribly dangerous if she did. The valley didn't belong to us anymore, he said. Whatever was going on there was beyond our control and certainly none of our business.

One day a farmer from Vaihingen who had always taken part in the Christmas shoot my father held each year stopped by to see us. Some of the fields near the construction site belonged to him, and he wanted to know what on earth was going on there. Although people had been barred from the site, everyone was talking about it; also, there were engineers and OT men quartered in the city. "What's it supposed to be, anyway?" asked this farmer. "Some cockeyed scheme, I'll bet — do they think *that*'ll win the war?"

Mother became very close-mouthed. She seemed to be completely preoccupied. One could see that she was planning something, but whatever it was, she kept quiet about it. One day she contacted the rationing office and offered to deliver some more food to the camp if they would send her another detachment of prisoners. Then she paid a call on the camp commandant and took me with her.

The commandant lived near the camp in a spacious barracks next to the pump house. The guards let us in through the gates, and after glancing nervously toward the watchtowers, we knocked at the commandant's door. We were admitted by an imposing Russian woman with a handsome face, high cheekbones, and a full mouth; but her eyes were small and dark, her glance piercing. She looks like a *Katya*, I thought. I had heard talk about *Katyas*, women who looked after the needs of soldiers behind the lines. They were also sometimes referred to as "bedside rugs."

So this *Katya* opened the door for us and showed us into the room where the commandant was sitting at his desk. He was, I believe, a major. In any case, he was part of the regular army, not the SS. A slight man, sporting a walrus mustache, he greeted us very politely as we came in. I could see mother sizing him up. In my basket I had some bread and liverwurst as well as a bottle of schnapps, which everyone knew was a vital commodity during wartime.

Mother began the conversation cautiously: "What kind of camp is this?"

"This is a labor camp for the construction site. We were transferred here from Poland."

"How many prisoners do you have?"

"At the moment there are about twenty-five hundred in the camp, plus guards. Unfortunately," he added, "the health of the prisoners is not very good. Everything is in such short supply. Worst of all, we've run out of coal for the delousing station."

He poured himself a second glass of schnapps, gulped it down gratefully, and said, "I really have nothing to do with the camp itself. I've merely been assigned to the administration here. The SS is responsible for the prisoners."

During the conversation the *Kapta* remained in the room, busying herself with one thing and another, and the commandant did not order her out. He said his family didn't live very far away, but he was rarely able to visit them. Then he offered to show us the building outside the camp. He took us to a large barracks, the delousing station, and wooden houses where the guards lived. We saw the canteen from the outside and went past the cave near the pump house — the cave we had often explored as children when we were feeling brave. There were bars across it now and we could hear dogs barking. We passed a few prisoners, who, when they caught sight of the commandant, stiffened and yanked off their caps. An SS man also came by, as if by chance, and accompanied us. He had a wolfhound on a short leash and a whip dangled from his belt. The commandant fell silent and returned with us to his office.

Mother approached the subject carefully. Could the commandant send us another work detachment so she could fulfill the demands of the rationing office? For a moment he hesitated, then agreed.

On the way home, mother became reflective. "A weak man, that commandant," she said. "He must have gotten into trouble in the army; otherwise, he wouldn't be here. Maybe it'll be possible to work with him." We had already passed Hermann Schneider's house when she said, "If we got some prisoners, we could build up their strength. We could find out what was going on in the camp, and maybe we could even save them."

Because the commandant needed straw urgently before winter started and because our name was so well known that we were above suspicion, one day thirty prisoners in clogs appeared again in the courtyard. It was the same detachment of men that had been sent to us before.

I was to take the guards to the room where the servants ate. "Give them a proper lunch," said mother. With a fearful look in her eye, Josepha served them sausages and bread. Some of the guards had stayed outside with the prisoners Szigmund was supposed to take to the bean field, but Szigmund remained in the hallway, rooted to the spot, and shook his head. "I won't have nothing to do with Jew." Felix and Janek nodded their agreement.

"But why not?" mother wanted to know. "They're prisoners just like you."

Felix exploded. "We are not Jews. I am good man, I always work hard, I won't go with Jews!" There was nothing we could do to persuade them.

So the Alsatian, who normally worked in the stable, was sent with the guards to see that the prisoners got to the bean field. Food would be brought out to them there.

It wasn't long, however, before the Alsatian was back again. "I can't watch that," he said to mother, his voice trembling. "They're beating the poor devils. It's not right."

The prisoners made a sorry sight in the bean field. They tried to find beans on the bushes, but couldn't. Their baskets would topple over or they'd trip on them. Then the guards would begin cursing and would strike the prisoners with their rifle butts. Mother told everyone to stop working and said that nobody would be beaten here. She showed the prisoners how to pick the beans, and gradually things settled down in the field. The guards sat in the grass. We brought out potatoes, bread, and cottage cheese to the prisoners and watched as they devoured it all with voracious speed and trembling hands.

So it went for a whole week. The Poles were put to work elsewhere on the farm. The guards didn't beat the prisoners anymore and even got used to not keeping a particularly close eye on them. Gradually the guards began to open up and talk about themselves a bit. Most of them had come from Siebenbürgen in Rumania, where a large group of Germans had settled during the eighteenth century. They were proud of belonging to the German minority in a foreign country and proud of their well-kept farms, fine wines, and the good crops they raised. Down through the generations they had protected their language and customs in an alien environment, and they believed wholeheartedly in the great German Reich. They had volunteered for the German army and had ended up in the SS before they had any idea what the SS was. Then they were assigned to the camps and never got away from them. One of the men, who had five children at home, even started to cry, saying it would have been better to have been killed at the front than to be stuck in this mess.

The Siebenbürgers were afraid of the "regulars," as they called them, especially one named Hecker. The "regulars" were a group of SS men who had had a lot of concentration camp experience, both at Camp Oranienburg and later at the camps in Poland. They were the cruel ones, the ones with dogs. Though few in number, they ruled the camp. And Hecker was their boss.

As time passed I learned to tell the prisoners apart. There was one who had a long, open sore on his leg which made a wet spot on his trousers. "Starvation edema," my mother called it. There was another named Macharowski, a large man with dark eyes and a squarish face. He had been a tailor in Danzig. But the first one who trusted me was a young prisoner from Hungary. He was clumsy and spoke only broken German. Once when the guard was at a distance, he pulled an old, yellowed photograph out from his shirt. "My father," he said. "Dead now."

"What makes you think that?" I asked.

"Maidanek," replied the Hungarian, glancing around nervously.

"What's Maidanek?"

"You do not know? Maidanek is camp in Poland," he whispered hoarsely. "Many thousand go in, then bottom drops out. Everybody dead." I thought he must be crazy.

I also learned what a capo was. Although they wore the same striped uniforms as everyone else, these prisoners could take a piece of bread away from the others without being punished. They earned special privileges by informing on their fellow inmates. If a capo were anywhere nearby, the others would clam up quickly.

Slowly I was drawn into the world of the prisoners. Without really being aware of it, I lost interest in anything not connected with the camp. It became the only thing that held importance for me.

When the beans had all been picked, the fruit in the orchards became ripe and the prisoners started working on the apples. Each was assigned to a tree and given a ladder. The Alsatian and I helped them get started, then they were on their own for the rest of the day. They were already growing stronger; even the sores caused by malnutrition had slowly begun to heal. The prisoners walked with a steadier gait, and we thought we saw the dull, sickly look in their faces giving way to a somewhat better color. They sat in the trees, soaking up the autumn sunshine, and methodically loaded their bags with apples, a few of which they ate. It was easier to talk to them now. We learned that most of them originally came from Poland and either had lost contact with their families or knew they were no longer alive. Fear never left the prisoners' eyes. "We are just subhumans," they would sometimes mutter during conversations. In the evenings they took as much food as they could hide back to their comrades in the camp. They stuck pieces of bread and potatoes down the legs of their pants, which were tied above the boots.

By now the air raids had grown so intense that the construction site had to be abandoned, and the work there given up. The cement mixers stood idle in the fields. The piles of cement sacks grew smaller, and the barracks containing construction materials were cleared out.

With the construction site closed down, Wiesengrund was turned into a camp for sick prisoners. This we learned from the men in our work detachment. They told us that nightly transports brought increasing numbers of the sick and dying from other camps all over Europe.

Whenever mother passed close by the camp, the prisoners would come out of their barracks and stand expectantly at the barbed-wire fence. Mother would walk slowly on, with her hands thrust into her jacket pockets. Her thoughts centered on the camp.

After some weeks she decided the time was right to try to find out what was actually going on inside. Macharowski, the tailor, who had been given Hanne's old room in which to mend clothing and patch towels, had become mother's confidant, for the guards had gotten used to leaving him pretty much alone there. She asked him which of the prisoners in the camp were the leaders. Macharowski said they were the doctors — among others a Belgian called Bongarz and a Norwegian named Poulsen.

"Poulsen, Poulsen," mother mused repeatedly. "Didn't Henrik have a friend in Oslo by that name?" Henrik was her brother and a physician. She decided to write to him about Dr. Poulsen. Because Uncle Henrik had been sent to the eastern front to deal with an epidemic of spotted fever, it was a long time before she received an answer from him. Finally he responded that he had indeed known a Dr. Poulsen in Oslo. He had heard that Poulsen's son, also a physician, had been arrested for being anti Quisling* and had disappeared.

So mother sat down and addressed a letter to Dr. Poulsen, Camp Wiesengrund. She explained how she had heard of him and asked him about the camp, how it was organized, how one could help, and whom one could trust. Macharowski smuggled this piece of paper, folded up very small, into the camp in his boot. Mother knew that by sending the letter she had put her life into the hands of a prisoner. What did she actually know of him except that he had quiet ways and serious, trustworthy eyes? Now she waited anxiously to see what would happen next. She was convinced that with the Allied armies approaching, sooner or later the order would be given to liquidate all the camp inmates. She hoped that when that time came the commandant would oppose the order.

Mother had also established contact with the official camp physician. Dr. Dischmann was a thin, young SS officer with a soft face who had stopped in our courtyard a few times. He assured mother everything possible was

---

Vidkun Quisling: Norwegian politician who betrayed his country to the Nazis and became its puppet ruler.

being done to improve the prisoners' state of health. He seemed sympathetic, yet I couldn't bring myself to believe him.

One day mother got a letter that had been smuggled out of the camp in Macharowski's boot, but it wasn't from Dr. Poulsen. Written in tiny handwriting, in French, this letter was from a Catholic priest who asked for hosts and gave explicit instructions how they should be baked. He said many people were begging for the last sacrament as they lay dying. The letter was signed by a Père de la Perrudière from Tours, France.

Mother was taken aback. This was hardly something she had expected, but we went ahead, baking the hosts according to the directions and giving them to Macharowski to take back to the camp. We thought it would be a miracle if they ever got into the hands of the priest, but it turned out that they did. We also tried smuggling aspirin and cheese, for protein, into the camp in the pockets and trousers of those prisoners we trusted. But our efforts to help the twenty-five hundred prisoners in Wiesengrund must have seemed like a teardrop falling into the sea.

At last an answer came from Dr. Poulsen. That night, after all the shutters had been closed, mother read the letter several times. It shattered all her hopes. "Save yourselves," it read. "We are lost already. Illness and hunger are raging in the camp. We have typhus and cholera and no medicine. There is no salvation. Thank you for your concern, but as for us, we no longer have any hope."

Mother wept as she read it. She had hoped that if one could work with people inside the camp, the guards might be put out of action and the prisoners saved. But Dr. Poulsen's letter crushed all hope of this plan working.

The guards became increasingly aloof, a sign that the camp administration suspected something. But it seemed they didn't dare cut off our detachment of workers yet, especially since we were still delivering food to the camp.

One time when the prisoners were working in the field at some distance from one another, I found myself standing next to a man I didn't know yet. He was new to the detachment. Suddenly I saw him look past me with eyes wide open. SS leader Möller was coming across the field with a whip in his belt and his wolfhound at his heel. Möller had started coming more often lately to check up on what the prisoners were doing. He was very close behind me. The prisoner trembled and his hands went limp still clutching the shovel handle. "Can't you give a salute?" bellowed Möller. But the man froze. Möller then raised his whip and struck the prisoner right in the face. The prisoner screamed and doubled over, pressing his hands to his face. By the time he straightened up again, Möller was gone, but something had happened to the man's face. His chin had been dislocated and his cheeks were swollen out of shape and beginning to turn purple. That had been no dog's whip but one with steel at the tip. The prisoner picked up his shovel and very slowly began to work again. I felt sick. The prisoner never came back after that day.

The young man who had spoken up when we first gave the prisoners potatoes was part of the detachment for many weeks. We learned that his name was Jakob. Whenever possible, mother tried to get work for him away from the guards so she could talk to him. He had impressed her most of all. He was always calm, polite, and quiet. He also spoke German almost without an accent. The other prisoners treated him with great respect, as though he were someone special.

One day mother returned from the fields very excited. "Jakob asked me whether I could hide him and then help him escape," she said. We considered all the possibilities. We could fix up a hiding place for him in the hayloft above the rafters at the back of the barn, but the dogs would discover him there. Or we could drive him away in the tractor trailer, but then there were the Poles. . . . If we tried to save him, we would ruin any possibility of helping the other prisoners. Everything would fall apart. No, we couldn't risk it.

Later I saw mother looking through the bookshelves. "Jakob asked me for a book. What kind of book can I give to a man in such a situation?" My father thought only the Bible would do, but the New Testament was the book of the Christians. In the end, the best book mother could find was a small, beautifully bound volume of Jacob Burckhardt's *Reflections on World History.* But what good would reflections on world history do him now? For him and for us, world history had reached point zero. He asked only that once about escape and afterwards never mentioned it again. He took *Reflections on World History* into the camp, hidden under his shirt.

When it became cold outside and the sun no longer cut through the fog, mother let the prisoners work in the greenhouse, where it was warm. They would sit at the long tables and transplant seedlings into the peat pots Josef had turned out on the machine. The guards sat around the boiler and a few even started reading. The greenhouse became like an oasis.

Nonetheless, two prisoners went berserk during those weeks. One of them suddenly got up from the table and began wrapping wire around his arms and legs. He sat on a pile of peat moss and wound wire all about himself with an ecstatic look on his face. The others tried to reason with him and to extricate him from the wire, but he just grinned and kept on wrapping himself up. The guards looked on and shrugged their shoulders but took no action. The following day he didn't come back.

Another prisoner started raging and foaming at the mouth. He pounded on one of the long, wooden tables with his fists, screaming words we couldn't understand and flailing about with his arms until the guards tied him up and took him away.

My father kept his distance from all this, seeing enough of it to shake his head as if to say it was more than he could fathom. One time I was watching him as he stood before the mirror shaving. He made a white beard out of shaving cream and said, "I seem to be some kind of fossil. Imagine, I was born in 1877 and

13

*O*ne day the news reached us that my brother, having survived the Battle of Narva, lay in a Red Cross hospital with typhus. His comrade, a Finn, had found him lying unconscious, had loaded him into an armored truck, and had driven eleven days with the Russians at his heels before coming to a place from which my brother could be shipped to Germany.

When he came to visit us from the hospital for the first time, he looked pale and hardly said a word. However, he added a second poem cut out of the newspaper to the door of mother's office:

> It was the numbness of grief.
> Flames reaching up like a giant hand.
> Empty beyond belief
> lay the land.
>
> Forests with branches wizened
> savage and sere
> forge a singular vision
> of the remains of all we hold dear.

Skeletons jutting and bare
no longer leaves adorn.
A symbol everywhere
that a bloody dominion was born.

Flowers choked by thorn.
Hatred and wrath worldwide.
Rustling fields of corn
drooped and died.

By the time we discovered this poem, my brother had
already gone back to the hospital. Although we had told
him about the camp, he had not been down to the grove
to see it himself. The poem was meant to convey his
own war experiences to us: the retreat from the siege
of Leningrad, the front lines along Lake Peipus, and the
Battle of Narva. And yet it seemed to capture our feelings
about the camp in the valley.

Just why mother went to call on the Catholic priest
in a neighboring town, I don't remember. Perhaps she
wanted to persuade him to perform a marriage ceremony for two of our workers. (Foreigners were prohib-
ited from marrying, and it was very difficult to obtain
permission for them to do so.) Or perhaps she just
wanted to pour her heart out to someone, and this priest
was said to be a good and wise man. She insisted I
accompany her even though I didn't want to. I felt I
didn't belong anywhere anymore and could not and
would not listen to someone preaching about the kind-
ness of God.

Despite my hesitation, the priest did succeed in making an impression on me. He listened sadly, shaking his head at what mother described. But what was so hard for me to understand was his telling us that even this would pass. After the war, everything would get better, he said, and a decent Germany would emerge from the ruins. He was the first and only person I met who envisioned a time after the war. I could not imagine that what now governed our lives would ever come to an end, nor could I imagine what would follow. The Catholic priest seemed to me like a voice crying in a vast wilderness. And I didn't believe him as he explained quietly that ·we would put these times behind us like a bad dream and that afterwards the world would be a different place.

Christmastime came. Christmas had always been the most festive time of the year. All the women of the village, including us, used to bake cookies of various kinds. Each family had a special recipe. The cookies would then be arranged nicely on plates and exchanged among the people in the village. The blacksmith got some, and so did the butcher and the farmers who lived in the upper lane. Special friends would receive a goose or a brace of hares from my parents with their Christmas greetings. On the morning before Christmas, the whole village — the houses and even the barns — was thoroughly cleaned and the roads swept. Then the men would go to the woods to cut a Christmas tree. The bakehouse would be filled with the aroma of freshly baked cookies.

This Christmas eve we had few cookies. But mother had the tables pushed end-to-end in the entrance hall and festively set. As evening approached, all the people who worked for us were called together and invited to sit at the table. At each place was a small gift. Candles flickered between evergreen boughs. They were all there: the Poles and Russians, the Ukrainian girls, Josef's son and Szigmund's baby. At the head of the table sat my father with mother on one side of him and me on the other; next were the Alsatian and his wife. There was hot cider spiced with cinnamon and cloves. Josepha had prepared a traditional Polish Christmas stew adding dried pears, of which we still had plenty, and peas. After dinner, mother spoke. She thanked all of the workers for their hard work and loyalty. She said the war would soon be over and then they could all return to their homelands and rebuild their lives. She broke into tears, as she always did when she was moved. Father said a prayer. Since there was no one Christmas carol all of us knew, the girls sang a Russian song with many verses.

In the meantime, Szigmund and Franz had slipped away from the table. There was a knock at the door and in came two Santa Clauses with sacks tossed over their shoulders. Szigmund was wearing a beard made of cotton and, to our great surprise, he'd put on mother's khaki jacket. He set his sack down on the floor, saying that he was Saint Nicholas and had come all the way from America. Peace was coming right behind him. Maybe it was a little late, but by Easter, peace would definitely be here. Then across the table decked with candles he shouted loudly, "Dobre, dobre, Wielkanoc" ("Happy, happy Easter"). We felt rather lighthearted as the men and girls left for midnight mass in the Vaihingen church.

It was after Christmas when the epidemic broke out among the prisoners. They sat at the long tables in the greenhouse, putting the tiny plants into pots. I was going along the line, removing full pots and replacing them with empty ones, when I came to a prisoner who was sitting all hunched over.

"Are you sick?" I asked, and looked at his face to find that it was covered with red spots. His lips were raw and cracked, his eyes glassy with fever. He was frightened.

"Please," he mumbled, "please no say anyone." I helped him toward a post so that he could lean against it, but his head kept falling forward. There was a small house next to the greenhouse and I asked two other prisoners to help me take the sick man there without the guards noticing. They carried him along a path between the cold frames and into a room with a cot in it. We laid him down and covered him with a blanket. He was thirsty, so I gave him some water.

"Spotted fever," muttered one of the prisoners who had helped carry him. "If the SS finds out about it, we'll all be shot."

Mother, who already knew about the fever in the camp, came to look at the man. "It's contagious and terribly dangerous," she said. "You mustn't stay here." I had heard that this was the kind of typhus most feared by our soldiers in the field, but I wasn't concerned for myself and strangely enough mother let me stay. She seemed too upset about the state of affairs in the camp even to worry about me getting sick. For the next two days, the man was dragged from the camp to the greenhouse and then brought to the room to lie down on the cot. I'm sure the guards noticed, but they didn't try to stop us. Every so often I went to give him water, and I could tell by his feverish eyes that delirium had set in. Then one day the others stopped bringing him. I think they killed him so the guards wouldn't find out about the fever. Later I burned the blanket he had used.

14

*E*nemy airplanes were striking at night with increasing regularity. When the air raid sirens sounded, we'd go outside to see where the planes were attacking. This was fairly easy to determine because they first dropped "Christmas trees." These were red or green flares attached to parachutes which would drift slowly to the ground, illuminating and outlining the attacker's target. Then we'd see the bright puffs of exploding antiaircraft shells. It wasn't wise to stay outside too long when the target was in the vicinity because of the danger of flying shell fragments.

On one particular winter evening we were sitting together in the living room when the sirens at the railway station and on the roof of the mayor's office began wailing long and loud. Soon afterwards we heard the noise of approaching aircraft. In the west, flares were being dropped very close to us in a large square pattern. The Poles dashed outside and hid in the dugouts, while we ran up to the orchard and jumped into the Tobruk shelters. I had the lid of mine raised slightly and was peeking outside when, slowly and ponderously, a low-flying plane came over the treetops, looking like a large, swaying bird. I could see its dark shadow through the branches. It must have been an old plane. Just like a big pigeon, I thought. Mother stuck her head out of the next bunker and shouted at me, "The 'Music of the Spheres' is about to begin.* Take cover!"

More and more planes flew over. The antiaircraft guns at the railway station began firing. It was obviously going to be a major attack. In the distance there was a rumbling sound like sacks of potatoes rolling down a chute. Explosions followed, one after the other, causing the ground to shake. Night fighters stationed at the nearby airport took off. There were dogfights taking place right over our heads. I saw one plane get hit and go down in flames. Flares flickered red and green and floated to the ground. To the west of us a bright reddish glow spread over the nocturnal skies. For a while there were intermittent explosions; then the sound of airplane motors receded as things quieted down again. Finally there was nothing left but the reddish glow in the sky. The attack had lasted less than half an hour, yet in that short time Pforzheim, only twelve miles from us, had been completely flattened.

A war widow left alone with a young daughter used to come to help my mother out in the office. She lived in Pforzheim and would come by train, provided the

---

"Music of the Spheres": A waltz by Johann Strauss.

tracks hadn't been bombed. The morning after the air raid, mother sent Josef and me to the city to find out whether the woman was all right and to tell her that she could stay with us if her home had been hit. We took the tractor so that on the way back we could get a load of fertilizer from a freight car that had been stranded on a side track. It was a cold day and although I had a blanket spread over my lap, I just couldn't get warm.

The smell of smoke permeated the whole region. When we came to the edge of the city and crossed the bridge over the Enz, Josef suddenly slammed on the brakes. Rubble lay everywhere, on the street and in the river. I jumped down off the tractor. Old, crusted snow lay at the sides of the road. Floating in the river between charred beams, boards, and pieces of ice were bodies. We drove farther into Pforzheim. People were trying to put out fires or were digging in the rubble that yesterday had been their homes. Some were wandering around in a state of shock. We asked how to get to the street where this woman lived. But we couldn't find her house. It was no longer there; there was nothing there except piles of rubble. No one we asked could tell us anything about her, so finally we turned around and started home. Josef said nothing. I felt colder than I had ever felt in my life. Later we learned that the woman and her little girl had perished in the ruins.

As I peered down from the bridge into the river, I thought of Rolf Potmann. During one of his visits, he'd told us how he had flown with his squadron over the

Thames in one of the first air raid attacks on London. He described in detail how they had flown into the city at daybreak along the river, cruising only a few meters above the water. It was in this way that they had been able to elude the warning system and come by surprise. Rolf related how they had suddenly swooped up off the water and into the heart of London, where they had dropped their bombs. He described it as a great and daring mission for the German Luftwaffe. But he didn't drive through the rubble his bombs had left behind. He didn't stand on the bridge afterwards and look into the water to see corpses drifting by, or stop at the edge of the road where frozen bodies could not be distinguished from dirty snow. When I saw all this, Rolf Potmann had been dead for a long time. And this wasn't the Thames, but our own little river, the Enz.

The main railroad track, which went past the old vineyard, was continually being bombed. The trains were halted while Russian prisoners of war made the necessary repairs; then they would proceed on. The plaques on the cars proclaimed: "Wheels must roll for victory."

One morning there was a great to-do in the village. "Haven't you heard?" people were shouting to one another. "There's a train sitting on the tracks right at the crossing. It's a long freight train from France." All the villagers began hitching up their horses. Our Poles couldn't be restrained from going either. Felix asked to use the horse and cart. Szigmund took the girls with him. Even Emma Linkenheils got out her little rack wagon and went off down the road. And old Mathilde went with her wheelbarrow, which she normally used for gathering rabbit fodder along the roadside. People came from neighboring villages as well.

The scene at the train was chaotic. People were climbing into the boxcars and pulling everything out. Many things had been thrown onto the ground and had gotten trampled in the mud. Tempers flared. People shoved and swore at each other. It was as though they were all intoxicated. The soldiers accompanying the train had orders to stop any looting, but after seeing the expressions on the faces of the looters, they just looked the other way. The atmosphere was full of tension; it was dangerous for those who tried to take too much, but just as dangerous for those trying to guard the train. It was a bad experience for the village, one nobody would talk about later. But afterwards scarves and aprons, summer dresses and skirts, all made out of the same black, flowered material, appeared everywhere.

15

*A*s 1945 progressed, the sun passed higher in the sky and shone strongly through the panes of the greenhouse. The plants in clay pots already had their second set of leaves and would be ready to set out in the fields around Easter time. Every morning I walked to the nursery, going past the milk depot and out along the field path, whose grassy banks were already turning green. I'd already helped with the milking before breakfast and had given the newborn calf water. I felt that this calf was really mine because I had been present at its birth, had cleaned it off with straw, and had given its mother a dose of bran to strengthen her.

After the girls had opened the vents of the cold frames, the prisoners arrived with their guards to do the now familiar work. They sat at the edge of the flats, slowly and carefully sticking the tiny plants into the soil. If the guards were far enough away, I could sit among the prisoners and talk to them. I had already learned about Maidanek, but it was in the cold frames that I first heard about Auschwitz. "They are giving soap and also towel, they are making thumb up or down, there is child and woman and man, they are standing in rows many hundred deep, they are going through big gate and big hall, they are making gas on, then is dead, woman and child and man. . . ."

The inmate named Jakob had already told my mother about Auschwitz. He had come to Camp Wiesengrund from there, after being selected for work. Macharowski also talked about Auschwitz, and about the ghetto in Warsaw. In Warsaw the Jews tried to escape through the sewers, but the SS and Polish militia were waiting at the exits and killed them as they came out. Quietly, while he continued sewing, Macharowski told us how they had shot his wife right in front of him as he stood waiting to be transported.

The people in the village looked on with mixed emotions as the detachment came to work every morning. "Poor devils," said Frau Seizinger, wiping her brow. One or another of the village women was always slipping them something on their way back to the camp. Families whose sons were prisoners of war in Russia hoped someone would take pity on their own sons if they were shuffling along somewhere like these men. On the other hand, the villagers couldn't understand why my mother continued to request this work detachment when we had enough, and certainly more efficient, help to do the work. The villagers couldn't get close enough to see the camp, so they had no way of knowing what was actually going on in the valley. The fields around it had been blocked off and the trainloads of new prisoners always arrived at night. That the procession up to the old clay pit grew longer by the day, that seventy or eighty stretchers were now carried up there every morning could only be seen from the path through the grove, and we were the only ones permitted to use it.

As spring came, snowbells blossomed in the woods and the forsythia hedges opened their yellow buds — but in the west the low rumble of big guns could be heard. Although people at the milk depot talked about thunderstorms, everyone knew it was the front coming closer. Mother hoped that somebody — anybody — would take the initiative and try to make peace with the Western Allies, but who could do it and, in any case, the Allies were no longer in the mood for peace.

The construction site lay deserted. The barracks around it stood empty. The OT men had vanished. Mountains of cement sacks and rusty iron beams were scattered in the fields. On the floor of the quarry the iron pilings rose toward the sky as before, but the ladders on the walls were falling apart. The rusty little "Baresel and Sons" sign still hung on the wire fence.

But mother had formulated a new plan. The idea had come to her at the construction site when she saw the empty shafts that had been intended for use as underground runways. She presented her plan to the camp commandant, imploring him to save the inmates by seeing that they got into the shafts before the SS received orders to liquidate them. The occupying forces, she said, would be the Americans, who were already just outside

Cologne. In return, everybody from the vicinity would vouch for him when the Americans came. For our part, she explained, we would secure the shafts with solid steel air raid doors. They surely could be found somewhere. We would also supply food to the shafts so that the prisoners could hold out there for several days. Then at least they could be defended against the SS guards. The invasion of the Allies was imminent and the commandant knew it. He agreed to the plan and pledged to cooperate with my mother.

So the Poles began fitting the entrances to the empty shafts with antiaircraft doors. We brought down straw and sacks full of dried pears and beans. These bunkers were enormous, wide enough for an airplane to pass through and so deeply blasted into the rock that water seeped down their sides. Four or five such tunnels had been created before work was suspended. Our workers knew that these bunkers were going to provide a good shelter for them, but they knew nothing about the plan for the camp inmates.

It was a lovely spring. Even February had been warm and sunny. The clumps of earth in the plowed fields dried up and broke apart easily when kicked with the toe of one's boot. The farmers went out with their harrows to prepare the ground for sowing. The plants in the greenhouse were ready to be set out. For the first time on the Swiss radio station, I. R. von Salis was speaking about an end to the war.

One day a radio truck from an antiaircraft unit pulled up to the house. It stood there in the middle of the

courtyard in the noonday sun looking large and conspicuous. Mother conferred with the officer in charge.
She told him that in no time at all his radio truck would
become a target for the enemy aircraft that filled the
sky above us. But the truck was out of gas; so everyone
pitched in, pushed it out to the field barn, and covered
it with bales of straw. The soldiers were relieved; only
the officer questioned whether he should have gone
ahead and used the radio in the middle of the day from
the center of our courtyard.

Groups of forced laborers began passing through the
village — men and women coming from factories that
had been bombed out. They wanted to work in exchange
for some food. They wandered aimlessly through the
streets and camped in the straw out in the field barn.
Twelve million such prisoners and forced laborers were
working in Germany toward the end of the war.

One evening a group of about twenty Russians stood
before our house. The women wore padded smocks and
had babushkas tied around their heads. One carried a
small child in her arms. Their spokesman was a tall,
gaunt man who knew some German. He requested shelter for all of them. The barracks and factory buildings
near Karlsruhe, where they had worked, had been gutted
by fire, he said. "Everything kaputt," he said. "No eat,
no work, no room." The Reich had started to collapse
— that was apparent.

Mother could not bring herself to let these people go
off into the night again, so she sent them to the house

in the nursery and we fixed some soup for them. "They can stay here till it's all over," she said.

A company of German infantry on its way to the front was quartered in the village. We discovered that a cousin of ours who'd been drafted at the eleventh hour was in this group. With the war all but lost, our cousin had no desire to go on fighting. Mother told the commanding officer that this soldier was very sick. She even wrote a letter describing his symptoms. By the next morning quite a few of the men in the group had disappeared. When the remainder of the company pulled out, our cousin stayed behind in bed. Later he set out towards home. "Well, at least one made it," mother commented dryly.

After those soldiers had left, older men wearing patched uniforms came to organize the Volkssturm* in our area. Every night those men still remaining in the village, the young boys, and the women had to erect barricades across the roads and plant explosives on the bridges leading into the village. Old man Schneider had to do it and so did Farmer Kühner and the Trostels. Under the command of aging sergeants, they rebuilt the bridge over the creek which had been hit by bombs. I suspect that during the day old Schneider and Trostel secretly removed the explosives they had had to plant the night before.

March was so warm that we could already start plant-

*Volkssturm: A territorial army formed by the Germans in the latter part of World War II, consisting of men and boys unfit for regular military service.

ing potatoes. We sorted through mounds of them, taking the small ones to the fields and carrying the larger ones to the bunkers at the construction site. The fruit trees in the orchard began to bloom. Every day I walked along the tracks of the local train to the bunkers. When Felix arrived with the cart, we would unload the food and cover it with straw. We even built a makeshift stable in the bunker in case we had to bring the cows there.

Macharowski, the tailor, had been working by himself in the gardener's house for so long now that the guards more or less ignored him. He was supposed to be patching bed sheets, but during the final days when the prisoners came to the nursery, mother gave him a special assignment no one else was to know about. For this assignment he needed some bright-colored cloth, which was almost impossible to come by in those days. But then I remembered the flag.

The girls from the Women's Labor Corps had left some time ago. With the situation growing more and more chaotic, they had decided to try to make their way home by one means or another — by bicycle, by train (if there was one), or on foot. The big house now stood empty — swept clean, its shutters closed. But left behind, rolled up in a corner, was the large, bright-red swastika flag they had raised each morning. I took it to Macharowski, who cut letters out of it and sewed them onto the sheets.

Mother kept herself somewhat informed about the position of the various Allied armies by listening to von Salis's broadcasts. She was certain we would be occupied by the Americans under General Patton. Since the commandant had promised to take the prisoners to the shafts, she wanted to draw the attention of the occupying troops to them quickly by hanging a conspicuous sign from the stone wall of the river valley. A large banner with red letters was fashioned under Macharowski's skillful hand. It declared in less-than-perfect English:

HERE ARE 2,000 MEN IN GREATEST DEPRESSION.
COME AND HELP.

As the roar of artillery grew louder and louder, people at the milk depot no longer spoke of thunderstorms. At night small groups of German soldiers could be seen walking along the field paths. Father thought that the Enz would be one of the last lines of defense and that German troops would make a final stand somewhere in our area; so we began to bury our old silverware and other valuables.

Then one day the prisoners stopped coming to us. It looked as though the commandant was going to keep his word. Mother was the first to observe the lines of inmates going from the camp to the shafts. Accompanied by armed guards, they were moving in long rows and carrying sacks on their backs.

Mother became all excited and ran into the living room crying, "He's doing it!"

But father remained skeptical. "I'd be surprised if that man could be trusted," he said.

From a distance we watched the procession of people going to the shafts. We couldn't understand, however,

why those same stooped figures then returned to the
camp. Mother left to talk to the commandant, but when
she came to the first barricade across the path, the
guards wouldn't let her pass. In fact they shouted at
her, "Get out of here immediately," and lowered their
machine guns ready to shoot. Mother returned home
in despair.

The next day was Saturday and, as was customary
on weekends, all the carts were brought into the courtyard and placed in front of the barn — the small carts
with rubber tires, the large rack wagons, and the trailer
for the tractor. They all stood in a row, neat and clean,
and on Sunday morning they were still standing there,
as if resting in the sun from the heavy labors of the
week. Around noon we heard the shuffling of clogs, only
this time there were hundreds and hundreds of them.
Into our courtyard came prisoners loaded like mules
with bundles and knapsacks belonging to the guards.
Storm troopers, with machine guns in hand and dogs
barking on leashes, walked among them.

The bundles and sacks were loaded onto our carts.
Shrill commands rang out in the courtyard. Some of the
prisoners were ordered to man the drawbars, while the
others were made to push. Then this throng of prisoners
formed into a long line, slowly moving the carts past
the blacksmith shop up the main street. From the window we saw all our carts rolling away.

We ran outside. Mother was beside herself. "What are
you doing? What's going on here? Where's the commandant?" she shouted. The entire village was in an

uproar. One woman began to cry. The farmers came out of their houses into the streets. Father ran after mother to try to stop her. One of the storm troopers whirled around and came at her threateningly.

"We know *you*," he roared. "You're a traitor. I ought to shoot you on the spot." And with that he tightened his grip on his machine gun, his face twisted with rage. The people of the village shrank back in alarm. My father grabbed my mother by both arms and pulled her away. Two farmers had also stepped forward to protect her. She shook with anger as she watched the train of carts going off. Some of the prisoners pushing the carts turned around to my mother with helplessness and despair in their faces. With backs bent, they stared at us with empty eyes. That night we were informed that the prisoners were supposed to have been loaded into boxcars waiting at the main station, but they'd been forced to keep going because the tracks had been bombed out. Our empty carts had eventually been spotted at Bietigheim, fifteen miles away. Mother had lost. The Heckers and Möllers had won. And father had been right after all.

Afterwards I felt I had to get away and ran out towards the grove. It was already dark and planes were droning in the sky. I heard not a sound from our defenses. In the middle of the woods I suddenly found myself standing right in front of the local train. That's odd, I thought, it's never stopped *here* before. At the head of a long line of boxcars stood the steaming locomotive. I crept up the embankment, and from there

16

At the beginning of April the people of the village began to clean as though a holiday were coming. The Schneiders, the Linkenheilses, and all the others swept in front of their houses, put their pantries in order, and scrubbed their parlors. Something ominous was in the air. From time to time, isolated groups of German soldiers would pass through the village wearily pulling their artillery up the street. One such gun was set up near the park. The Poles observed all of this with skeptical looks on their faces. Mother took a bottle of brandy, which had been distilling during the winter months, and went out to the barn. "This estate has been here for over four hundred years," she said to the soldiers hunched down next to the gun. "Must it be destroyed now? Go on home; the war's over." And she gave them the bottle of brandy. A little while later the gun stood abandoned and the Poles went out and piled straw over it.

At the construction site I ran into a soldier who had just set up his field gun atop the rocky ledge overlooking the valley. "Wait till the others come," he warned. "*Then* you'll be sorry." On a hill on the other side of the Enz Valley I saw the white flag of surrender flying from the top of a house. The soldier noticed it too. "You women are in for a surprise," he said, and spat on the ground. But shortly after that he had gone, leaving the little field gun behind.

By the seventh of April all was quiet. There was no longer anyone in the fields. The roads were deserted. The Russian workers were sitting on the doorstep of the nursery. The wind blew across the *Weitfeld*, causing the firs at the corner of the nursery and the alders in the little woods to sway. Puffy white clouds drifted through the blue sky. In the valley the camp lay silent, unapproachable, and menacing — like a dangerous beast.

My parents decided to spend the next few days in the bunker because it looked as if there might be fighting near the village after all. We took all those who wanted to go with us and set ourselves up in the lower shaft. A group of people from Vaihingen had already occupied the upper one. They were amazed to find a huge pile of sacks containing dried pears and beans and other supplies there, including ammunition. This latter baffled us, too, until it dawned on us that the commandant had reversed mother's plan. Instead of moving the prisoners to the shaft, he had had them carry provisions there for the *guards*. Evidently the SS had planned to defend themselves in the bunker, but then for some reason had given up the idea.

The eighth of April dawned with a rose-colored sunrise, lifting the fog from the river valley. Flocks of crows came flying over the fields, which were planted with winter wheat. It was very early and everyone was still asleep when I crept up the ramp to the opening of the shaft. A young Russian named Lor was already there, crouching close to the ground. He pointed to a rounded hill on the other side of the Enz Valley, its crest illuminated by the first rays of the sun. Then I saw them for the first time — the *others*, a long, shimmering line of tanks pushing its way over the hilltop with guns directed at the construction site.

Suddenly I remembered the banner, which still lay rolled up inside the bunker. Lor and I ran back down to get it and also brought back two square poles that were lying nearby. No one else in the bunker was awake yet. We climbed up to the railroad tracks, cleared the stones away from under the rails with our hands, and pushed the two poles through. Then, tying the banner tightly to the ends of the poles, we pushed it over the edge of the quarry wall and let it unfurl. To be sure, there were no longer two thousand prisoners who needed help. Nor were they in the shafts, as had been planned. But there were at least several hundred of them trapped behind barbed wire in the camp, which was hidden in the valley behind us.

We lay flat on the tracks, watching the line of tanks

on the horizon move slowly forward. Not a single shot was fired. Only the gnashing sound of the treads was carried across the river valley on the wind. Then airplanes appeared in the sky and we heard artillery fire on the far side of the village.

We stayed in the shafts all that day. When night fell we saw a big fire on what seemed to be the Nussdorf Hills. People came running out to us from the village. "The French are here," they reported excitedly. "They're kicking in the doors and going in the houses. Your field barn is burning. They're strange characters, brown-skinned, and no one can understand a word they're saying. They're after the women. It doesn't matter how old, they're taking them all." My father counseled everyone to stay put and not to go back to the village. No one could do anything now but wait, he said.

When I heard that our barn was burning and no one was making any attempt to put the fire out, I thought to myself what cowards they all were, including my parents. So I sneaked out and ran along the tracks and across the field to the village. It was pitch black outside, a "cow's night," as father used to call that kind of darkness. But where Hermann Schneider's orchard bordered on the road, I could go no further. There were clanking, metallic sounds and I could hear strange, throaty voices. I crept on my belly almost to the edge of the road. There, silhouetted against the night sky, were soldiers and trucks moving along the road. The trees in the park stood out in the background, illuminated by the red glow of the burning barn. I heard women's screams coming from the village and the sound of rifle butts smashing against doors. A couple of shots rang out — thin, barking rifle shots. I dismissed all thoughts of putting out the fire. For a while, I lay there in the darkness under the trees; then I crawled back down the bank. Never in my life had I run as fast as I ran through the field that night.

When I got back to the bunker, they'd just noticed I was missing. "Where *were* you?" mother asked furiously. When I said I had been down by the road, she drew her hand back and gave me a resounding slap across the face.

"You deserved that," said my father. Then they sent for Josef, who always used to be the Poles' barber, and he sheared off my long, curly hair till it was as short as matchsticks.

The Poles were the first to leave the bunker the next day and I went with them. We climbed up the steep, stone steps to the railroad tracks. Our banner was still in place. A line of soldiers came toward us. The first one was carrying a machine gun and wore a brass helmet. He had a large, red mustache and shiny, coffee-colored skin. The Poles called and waved, pointing to the identifying patches they had to wear on their jackets. Josef threw his arms around the soldier with the mustache. The others laughed and offered us chewing gum and candy. One soldier, who had something tattooed on his dark, furrowed brow, embraced me.

The whole village looked very different. Foreign troops sat, stood, or crouched everywhere. Our courtyard was

full of tanks. The barn had stopped burning by now.
Soldiers were hauling pigs and cows out of their pens.
There was something cooking over a fire they had built
in front of the potato cellar. An officer who was leaning
against the doorway of our house, his cap askew, offered
his hand to Szigmund and asked in a friendly tone of
voice, "Do you belong here?" He spoke in German.

"Yes," answered Szigmund.

"I'm from Austria. We're the foreign legion." The officer was rather drunk and slurred his words.

Inside the house all the cupboards stood open and
some of the doors had been battered in. There were
guns and heavy military coats lying around. The mirrors
in the hallway had been shattered, and in the living
room a small fire was burning on the parquet floor.

My parents returned to the house a little while later.
There were hundreds of people milling around the courtyard. All the forced laborers who had worked for years
in our village were celebrating their liberation. They
were happily mingling and chatting with the French
soldiers. The Russians to whom my mother had given
shelter in the nursery were also there. All of a sudden
the tall fellow who was their spokesman recognized my
mother and came rushing up to her. Lifting her onto
his shoulder, he shouted, "Good woman, good woman."

Father greeted the Austrian officer, who in the meantime had slumped down on the bench in front of the
house. That he was Austrian and obviously drunk was
for my father a very human bridge to the new order.
So when father saw the shattered mirrors he started to

laugh. Standing among the foreign soldiers, he just laughed out loud. "I understand perfectly well why they smashed the mirrors — they saw their own faces in them."

There were soldiers sitting on the stairway, dozing or cleaning their rifles. There were even soldiers asleep in our beds. The poem about September and the one my brother had cut out were still hanging on mother's office door. And strangely enough — whether it was the lovely spring weather or the happy, excited laughter of our people — the whole thing struck me as a rather funny comedy.

Yet it was not funny at all. The farmers who'd remained in the village had been locked in their cellars by the French, who had also locked up my father for several hours. Farmer Kühner had been shot. He lay in the parlor of his house, which stood on the corner where the upper lane runs into the main street. He was dead. No one knew how it had happened, but apparently one of the Moroccan soldiers had killed him. Perhaps Farmer Kühner had been trying to protect his daughters. He was the only one in the village who did not survive the occupation by the French.

17

*C*amp Wiesengrund, however, had not yet been discovered by the French troops. The valley lay somewhat out of the way, hidden between the grove and the hillside where the clay pit was located. The camp was still sealed off and guarded by some of the SS men.

After three days had passed, mother decided that she had to bring the valley to the attention of the French. Asking to see the commanding officer, she was directed to old Schank's house, and I went along too. Because my hair had been cropped off and I was wearing Josef's big jacket with the *P* sewn on it, I felt quite safe from the foreign soldiers. There were orderlies posted in front of the French officer's quarters. A young lieutenant with friendly brown eyes stood at the doorway. He told us that no one was to be admitted; but after mother pleaded with him, he disappeared inside. A few minutes later we were shown into the family room, where an officer sat, hunched over some maps on the table. As we entered the room, he stood up slowly. He was a distinguished-looking gentleman with fine features and dark, wavy hair. In a chilly tone of voice he asked, "What do you want here?" In the French that she had learned as a child but had not used for many years, mother tried to explain that there was a camp down in the valley in which many prisoners had been locked up for days. She said that these people needed help right away and told him how to get to the camp. The officer listened in silence, then motioned us to the door with a flick of his head.

After we left the officer's quarters, we heard shots coming from the *Weitfeld*. There must have been a few German soldiers still holding out there.

Since there was no room for us at home, we decided to go back to the construction site. There we met up with an army jeep that was stopped on the road below the shafts. Two soldiers stood up in the open vehicle, looking at our banner through binoculars. They were photographing it and asked us what the sign was supposed to mean. Mother pointed toward the camp, which lay out of sight behind the trees.

These men turned out to be French war correspondents. They arrived at the camp just as it was being liberated by the French soldiers. Their account of what happened was published in the April 18 edition of the French military newspaper *Patrie*:

> The road running through the Enz Valley is lined with blossoming cherry trees. As one crosses a small bridge, the attention of the passerby is drawn to

a large, white banner hanging down into the valley
from an open quarry:

HERE ARE 2,000 MEN IN GREATEST DEPRESSION.
COME AND HELP.

it says in bold red letters.

A narrow, stony path leads to a camp composed
of about thirty weather-beaten barracks painted
grey-green. In the radiance of a sunny spring day
they look even more windblown and dilapidated.
The double barbed-wire fences and watchtowers
with spotlights remind us of many other camps.

We are immediately surrounded by hundreds of
emaciated prisoners in tattered, grey-striped concentration camp uniforms. A tall, haggard-looking
Pole shakes my hand and says in the best French
he can muster, "Long live France!"

In the distance we can still hear the sound of
heavy artillery and machine-gun fire and the in-
cessant droning of our airplanes, which are knocking out the last defensive positions of the enemy
one by one. We are in Vaihingen, seventeen miles
from Stuttgart.

In this camp there are no ovens and no gas cham-
bers. Here there is, to put it simply, only death:
death by starvation, by tuberculosis, by typhus. This
camp in Vaihingen was originally meant to be a
concentration camp for Polish Jews from Radom.
However, during their retreat in October 1944, the

Germans had to evacuate a large number of prisoners. That was how Camp Wiesengrund came to be. Those prisoners too weak or too sick to work were sent here. They came from all over Germany: from Neckarelz, from Trier, from Dachau. There had been as many as twenty-four hundred Frenchmen, Poles, Rumanians, and Russians here — without heat, without blankets, and naked under their uniforms. During the last winter they slept two to a cot to keep warm, covered only by a blanket of vermin. Countless numbers died of dysentery, of intestinal bleeding, of starvation, and of tuberculosis. Thirty every day. On top of all that, in January a typhus epidemic broke out. . . . Two thousand corpses were buried in pits around the camp. Those who hung on to life had to work, guarded partly by German SS and partly by French militia.

Thirteen hundred prisoners were left on April 1. The French troops were drawing closer and the Germans evacuated those who could walk, about six hundred. Six hundred and eighty have now been given their freedom. For many days they have had nothing to eat. At this sight I was reminded of the words of the Russian writer who said, "There are good Germans; they are dead."

After we moved back into our house, we found a copy of this newspaper and saw in it pictures of the camp. We had known a lot about the camp, but what it was really like even we could not have imagined. The French had liberated it by simply unlocking the gates and shooting the remaining SS guards or taking them prisoner. A long stream of humanity now began to wend its way out of the camp — deathly ill, dying, staggering, crawling. They came up the path to Hermann Schneider's house and down the village road to the inn zur Krone and Bausch's house; they came into the bakehouse and into our courtyard. They were everywhere, these scrawny figures in wooden clogs or bare feet. Their eyes were glassy, their faces the color of death. They were covered with sores and crawling lice. If I had not seen it with my own eyes — how they lay down on the side of the road and died; how they tried to catch a chicken, stumbled, and fell, never to get up again; how they sat in the road and ate sausages from the villagers' larders; how they yanked on Sunday suits and top hats belonging to the villagers — had I not seen it all myself, I would not have believed it. Those first steps into freedom taken by the survivors of Camp Wiesengrund were like something out of Dante's "Inferno," like the night-walking spirits of the dead.

Some of the men sat on the dunghill beside the horse stable and attempted to pluck a chicken. Another was riding a child's bicycle. He kept falling off, but with patience and tenacity he would get back onto the seat, which was much too low for him. A few crept into the machinery shed where some potatoes were stored and ate them raw. Others, overcome by weakness, simply fell onto the villagers' beds. And still others writhed with stomach cramps by the church wall. Some died with smiles on their faces, having filled their stomachs for the first time in years. They were friendly — no, they were completely indifferent to the Germans in the village. With gaunt faces that looked like skulls, they tried to eat, to put on clothing, to simply walk around. They dragged themselves among the intimidated villagers, who huddled together in rooms or remained crouching in their cellars. They crawled on top of overturned trunks and over personal belongings that had been trampled underfoot. Mother stood by in anguish and watched. "They've got to get some kind of medical help here. They can't just leave them like this!"

A whole group of prisoners entered our home and, searching from room to room, came upon a closet full of boots. Sitting down on the floor, they made a pile of boots and tried them on one by one to see which would fit. Mother stood nearby. She advised them not to eat too much, to let their stomachs get used to food first, and she offered to make them some soup. But they were so engrossed in the boots that they paid no attention to her. Then we heard someone yelling in the corridor and Jakob came through the door. He looked deathly pale. His prisoner's smock hung loosely from his shoulders, making his face look very thin, almost transparent. He looked around with his large grey-blue eyes and said to the men sitting on the floor, "What's going on here? Don't you know where you are? You'll take nothing from this house." Immediately obeying, the prisoners stood up without a word and went outside.

We sat down with Jakob and told him how happy we

were that he had made it. He said that when the SS
were clearing the camp of those who could still march,
he had pretended to be sick. He simply lay down on a
cot between a dying man and one who was already
dead. Hecker had called his name and even rolled him
over, but he'd just moaned. So they left him there. No
one had betrayed him and he was not shipped off with
the others. His plan now was to go to Poland to look
for his sister as soon as he'd recovered his health. He
thought it was possible she was still alive, though he
knew for certain that his parents were dead.

Warnings were issued about drinking the water,
which had already become contaminated; and indeed,
typhus did break out in the village. For days the weather
stayed hot and dry, increasing the danger of an epidemic. The spring sun shone down strong and golden.
All the bushes were in bloom. But there seemed to be
no relationship between heaven and earth.

Three days after the camp had been liberated, the
path to the quarry was still littered with the bodies of
dead prisoners. They were still dying in the villagers'
beds, yet no medical relief was forthcoming from the
French. So once again mother went to call on the officer.
The same young lieutenant with brown eyes admitted
us. The distinguished-looking officer stood up behind
the desk, reaching for his swagger stick as we came into
the room. He looked tired. Mother explained to him that
something had to be done and done fast. Typhus was
spreading, and the prisoners were dying like flies. We

Germans, she said, had to look on helplessly. Gently but firmly she implored him, "I'm asking you from the bottom of my heart, monsieur, to please save these people."

The officer cocked his head to one side and fixed his dark, narrow gaze on mother. "It's you, you Germans, who have perpetrated these atrocities. Don't come bothering me about it, madame." And with that he went to the door, flung it open, and pointed toward the street with his silver-knobbed stick. Then suddenly he recoiled, for there on the threshold, right in front of his door, knelt one of the prisoners. He had crawled there on his hands and knees, unobserved by the orderlies. As we were going out, he lifted his face to us, a face covered with sores, a skull-like face. His lips moved, but no sound came from them. We stared as the prisoner raised his hands to us in a suppliant gesture; then he collapsed in the doorway. Mother turned toward the officer, her eyes full of fury and despair. Without saying another word to him, we stepped over the crumpled figure and went back out into the road.

Not long after that, trucks came rumbling into the village to collect the prisoners. The French soldiers pulled them out of every corner, dragging them from houses and beds, barefoot or with only one shoe on, dressed in the jackets or pants of the villagers. They picked the prisoners up like sacks and tossed them into the waiting trucks, one on top of the other. Moaning, cursing, dying, they were transported back into Camp Wiesengrund, and the gates were locked behind them.

The local troop commander ordered the mayor of the village to come up with provisions for the camp's six hundred inmates within the next few hours or else he would be shot. Two junior officers came to get my mother to act as an interpreter. Mother wrote the following account of what happened that day:

The French took the mayor and me to the camp in an automobile. They let us out by the sentry box where the field path had been barricaded. The officers led us up a small, well-trodden path to the clay pit. It was there that we were suddenly confronted with the reality of Camp Wiesengrund. The officers removed their caps and stood in silence out of respect for the dead lying in the pit. Then one of them said to us, "It is your people who are responsible for these 'heroic' deeds."

They took us back to the edge of the camp where a sentry with fixed bayonet was posted in front of the gate. Suddenly a large prisoner came rushing at the fence, shook it violently, and screamed, "Whole families gassed and cremated, that's what you've done. I'll tear you apart with my bare hands. My little son — he was only three years old. My mother. My wife. You've killed them all." The officer only looked at us and said nothing.

We tried to get provisions for the camp. The mayor was supposed to mobilize all the Germans in the village to help, but many of the women and girls were still hiding in the shafts and he was having trouble finding enough people. I asked the Poles and Russians to come with us, but they were sitting in their lodgings with the Moroccan soldiers and the red wine was flowing liberally. At first they did not want to help, then they got up and joined us.

A woman came to us in tears saying that thirty soldiers had entered her house and seized some women. I begged the officer to go with me to the house to see what he could do. As we went in, there were soldiers pushing and shoving on the staircase. When they caught sight of us, they fled through the doors and windows. The family was an extremely pious one. In the small living room there were sayings from the Bible hanging on the walls. The women were dazed and bedraggled. Their clothes had been half torn from their bodies. We covered them as best we could and brought them back home with us. Though their eyes were still filled with terror, they came with us to Wies-engrund to help prepare a meal for the prisoners.

All the men of the village were ordered to help take the camp inmates to nearby hospitals and sanatoriums. They returned that night, horror-struck by what they had seen. "The sick on bare cots . . . hardly any blankets," the men related, "and those blankets were so full of lice they crawled. Even the bedbugs were eating the lice. We've never seen anything like it. We had to carry the dead men to the pit. They didn't weigh a thing

— just skin and bones. And we'll be the next ones to
be thrown into that camp."

That's what we all thought. We felt certain that the
French would put our whole village into the barracks
and close the barbed-wire fence behind us. But instead
the French set fire to the barracks. For two days and
nights they burned steadily, creating a thick pall of
smoke. Finally all that was left of the camp were charred
beams lying in the field. Everyone breathed a sigh of
relief. The valley was free again at last. A cross was
erected over the clay pit in memory of the twenty-five
hundred nameless people who were buried there. That
summer, red poppies bloomed all over the valley. There
had never been poppies in those meadows before — and
they bloomed there only that one year.

18

With the withering of the poppies, Camp Wiesengrund disappeared from the lives of most of us in the same way it had come, like a ghost or a bad dream. For most of us it had been just one more incomprehensible event at a time when fate toyed with people's lives as it pleased.

The grass sprang up again around the winding brook, and the pump house meadow lay empty. Soon the large quarry was back in operation and the farmers were out plowing those fields that had been enclosed by barbed wire. As soon as possible, we, too, began our spring plowing. And all those workers who'd been sent to us during the war helped us with it once again.

The first to leave were the twenty Russians who had come just before the Allied occupation. One day their spokesman showed up with a Soviet commissar. Together the two men rounded up all the Russians in the area and put them into camps in anticipation of the trip home. But as transportation was slow in coming, groups of Russians began roaming the countryside and became dangerous. If they came upon a German riding a bicycle and he did not hand it over immediately, they would shoot him.

The Poles were also waiting for the chance to go back home, but they were not sure whether they wanted to return to a homeland now occupied by the Russians. Josef was the first to leave. He and two other men hoped to get jobs with the American army. Wearing their good suits and each carrying a small suitcase, they came to say good-bye. The others stayed on. The plants were set out just as they had always been at that time of year. And, as usual, when we started watering the fields, the water pump in the nursery got clogged with weeds and had to be dismantled.

Then one day a truck carrying a commissar from Russia pulled up to the nursery. He had come to re-patriate the girls from Vilika Vovnianka: Lida, Sina, Nina, Maruscha — all of them. Only Szigmund's wife did not go with them. Barefoot, walking tall and straight, in long skirts with padded jackets over their shoulders and their possessions in bundles on their heads, the girls left as they had come. They did not laugh and they did not cry. "Dovizeni," they said softly, and climbed into the truck. As it pulled out into the road, they waved to us. We were very sad. For four years they had shared our life, and we had grown fond of them. Later we learned that they had not been returned to Vilika Vovnianka. Stalin was sending all those who had worked for the Germans, even though they had been forced to do so, to any place but their native villages. It was said that many were shipped to Siberia.

Bills were posted announcing that all German citizens had to turn in their weapons and firearms. The French soldiers went from house to house searching for them. In our village, weapons were supposed to be taken to the mayor's office. It was amazing what kinds of things turned up: machine guns that had been abandoned, revolvers from the Volkssturm, the hare-hunting guns that had long been Hermann Schneider's pride and joy. Father had to turn in his guns too, the ones he had buried in the park. Everybody knew about father's guns because 'all his life he had carried them through the village on his way to go hunting in the woods. When he brought them down, there was a crowd of people standing around the pile of firearms. Father was pale and his lips were tightly pressed together. Everyone watched as he took the guns out of the bag and dropped them, one by one, onto the pile. The last gun was an old one with his father's name inlaid in brass on the wooden stock. Holding this gun reverently in his hands, father looked around the room in desperation. Then, raising it high overhead, he hurled it against the wall, dashing it to pieces.

The French district officers treated my parents with civility. They even permitted us to use our automobile again. It was a very old one with a wood-gas generator* on the back. I was sent to the district office to have the

Wood-gas generator: A method devised during the war, when gasoline was scarce, of running an engine by converting wood into automobile fuel.

papers stamped. One needed permission from the military authorities for everything, so there were always long lines of people waiting in front of the town hall. On a bulletin board outside the office I saw the first German newspaper to appear after the war. It contained the latest news, public notices — and a poem, which I read and reread. Finally, when no one was looking, I tore it out, and it became the third poem fastened to mother's office door.

> A plowman tramps across the land
> And with his cool and ancient hand
> Plows up our earthly splendor.
> Across the land, through town and state,
> He pushes on his plow of fate
> And slowly turns us under.
>
> Quietly round him stand the woods,
> Quietly round him flow the brooks,
> The stars are silent spheres.
> So much precious time was spent
> In gossip and idle argument,
> Laughter and tears.
>
> Our worldly goods we leave behind us,
> Take off our shoes for they remind us
> Barefoot we must roam.
> The death and pain we've planted now
> Have burned their stamp into our brow.
> We shall atone.

So let them come — the sick, the poor —
Up the walkway to our door
And come without surcease,
So that we have forevermore
What their hearts are longing for —
A crust of bread
And simple mercies.

19

We heard that a German regiment had left hundreds of horses in a meadow near Ludwigsburg. Because the animals were starving, it was announced that people could come and take as many as they wanted. It must have been sometime in May, then, when Franz and I were sent to pick out some of these horses. When we got to the meadow, there were horses everywhere. Farmers were walking among them, and if they could get a horse to stand up, it was led away. The scrawny animals trotted after their new masters like lambs. Sitting on the edge of the meadow were a few German soldiers wearing old, threadbare uniforms. "We've come from Hungary," they said. "We wanted to save the horses. We didn't want to leave them behind for the Russians."

Franz and I picked out five: three white ones, a brown one, and a grey. With the horses in tow, we made our way along the paths through the fields to the Enz where the bridge crossing it had been destroyed. Only a few narrow planks had been placed across the piers, but the horses crossed this shaky footbridge without shying. When we got to the other side, Franz kissed their muzzles and exclaimed, "This is Arab. Arab like brother, like human." When we got home we tied the horses up in the large stable, which had stood empty since we handed our big Belgians over to the German army.

Now and then we received visits from former inmates of the camp who had been released from hospitals and were now waiting for emigration permits. Some of them wanted to go to Palestine, while others were preparing to immigrate to America. They told us about a group called Haganah that was organizing immigration into Palestine. They said the British were not letting the refugee ships pass and that there was fighting going on in Palestine over the land their ancestors had left centuries ago.

Some of them wanted to start an agricultural school in our area so they could prepare themselves for life in a kibbutz. Kibbutzim, they explained, were cooperatives with a twofold purpose, to till the land and to defend it.

We were just sitting down to eat one day when a former prisoner who had been part of the work detachment from the camp dropped by to see us. He was dressed in new clothes — a jacket that was too long for him, light-brown leather shoes, and a cap which he did not take off — and seemed in no hurry to immigrate anywhere. He wore a huge ring on his finger. When we invited him to sit down with us, he did not do so at once, but turned toward the tile stove, which stood in

the eastern corner of the room, and began to bow repeatedly, mumbling some kind of prayer. Each time he
bent over, his new leather shoes squeaked. Then he sat
down and began telling stories. He spoke in Yiddish,
which made understanding difficult for us, but his stories were nonetheless fascinating. He came many times
after that, always bringing something with him — a
tin of coffee or a piece of leather — which he offered
to exchange for sausage or butter.

Another camp survivor who visited us was Jakob, who
showed up one Sunday morning. His hair, by now grown
out, was jet black and his face no longer had that thin,
ghostly look to it. He was wearing tan riding breeches
and a dark green linen jacket, which he wore open over
his shirt. He and a friend of his named Oleg, who had
also been in the camp, said they wanted to go to
America. I didn't think that was right. Why wouldn't
they want to go to Palestine, the ancient land of the
prophets, to help create a new country there for the
Jews? A homeland of their own seemed like the only
possible safeguard against suffering such persecution
again.

It was a sunny morning and the bells were ringing
from the tower of our little church. The village looked
so clean and peaceful. Mother wanted to entertain our
visitors, and since I had already told the story about the
horses, she suggested a horseback ride. Thus it was that
I found myself riding to the woods with Jakob down
a trail that ran alongside the railroad tracks and was
bordered by a hedge of blackthorn. I was so happy. The

war was over and my brother had survived. I was almost nineteen years old; five of the nineteen had been war years. I felt like singing out loud. Then I thought of the man riding beside me, a man who had just come out of the camp, and the sound of shuffling wooden clogs came back to my ears. He had asked us to help him escape — had asked only once and then never again — but we had not been able to help. Each day he had gone back into the dreadful world of the camp. Jakob rode past me, breaking into laughter. He must have reined in his horse too sharply then, for suddenly it stumbled and fell. He lay on the ground beside the horse, and for one terror-stricken moment I thought Jakob had broken his neck. But to my great relief he got up, took the horse by the reins, and his large, grey, alert eyes briefly caught mine.

I don't recall exactly when we got the news that the French were pulling out and would be replaced by the Americans. But wherever French troops had been quartered, they were packing up and leaving. All their weapons were being loaded onto the train: trucks, guns, artillery. We heard they were being shipped to Indochina.

The captain of the military government in Vaihingen came to pay a farewell visit. My parents and he sat around the table and talked about Alsace, about Hartmannsweilerkopf,* where thousands of graves of French and German soldiers killed in the First World War lay

---

*Hartmannsweilerkopf: A battlefield in France, remembered for fiercely contested fighting between the Germans and French in the First World War.

facing each other. On one side the crosses read "Mort pour la France" and across the way "Sie starben für Deutschland." Now so many new graves had been added to these. The captain said that peace should finally be made between France and Germany, and my parents shared his hope that this peace would last forever.

The French priest who had sent the letter requesting hosts had also come to see my parents after being released from the camp. Before returning home, he wrote them a farewell letter:

> . . . I don't want to leave Germany without thanking you.
>
> I enjoyed your hospitality very much and was glad you were able to share my concerns about the future of our two nations. I did not want to be too optimistic about an early reconciliation, for that would not have been honest. I preferred only to indicate my sadness about the present situation. It will be a long time before the psychological conditions necessary for a reconciliation are present.
>
> Yesterday I was talking to a young soldier on the train platform. He said, "Now you explain this one to me. I have a comrade who got thrown into jail for two months just for getting into a fight with a German."
>
> "Maybe he was in the wrong," I suggested. "A wrong cannot go unpunished."
>
> "Why not? The Germans have certainly wronged us enough," he answered. I had a hard time con-

vincing him that this was no reason to justify evil.

But there are many well-intentioned people who are now working with great patience to secure a better understanding.

May this spirit prevail!

Everyone in the region expected a great deal from the American occupation. We heard they had everything: oil, canned goods, coffee, chocolate, powdered milk. They didn't come to our village at first, but entered Vaihingen, parking their jeeps and playing ball in the city square. They laughed a lot and chewed gum. People watched with astonishment as the Americans thoroughly disinfected the city milk depot. How much trouble they took to get the cans spotless and the milk purified! They certainly were different from the French.

They set up an American military government, which began to organize the administration of German towns and cities according to the principles of self-government. Instead of being appointed, mayors would be elected. Our village elected Trostel, the brother of Ottl and Fred the baker. Trostel, who had been a farmer all his life, now sat in the mayor's office buried under piles of paper, mostly applications for allotments of fertilizer, seed, oil, and ration cards. He was a slender, dark-haired, taciturn man and a good farmer.

The work in the fields and nursery now had to be done by unemployed laborers from the city and by discharged soldiers looking for room and board with farmers' families. Even a young Dutchman whose home was

on the Hook of Holland came to us. He was an excellent
gardener but hardly spoke a word, and mother thought
he might have served with the volunteer SS. He worked
doggedly and stayed with us for a long time.

Then the first German refugees began to arrive from
the East. They came in huge transports, as the girls
from the Ukraine had come not long ago, and carried
everything they still owned in boxes and old cardboard
suitcases. A family from the Sudetenland came to stay
with us; there were also a forester and his wife from
East Prussia, a family from Upper Silesia, and another
from the Lausitz region.* These refugees seemed confused and did not feel at home in our part of Germany.
For them the future was full of forebodings. Most had
been through terrible ordeals. They had been driven out
by the Poles or had fled in winter from the Russian
tanks, their homelands lost. They spoke nostalgically of
the little towns where they had grown up, of their beautiful fields, of their houses on the edge of forests where
the deer came at night. Their greatest fear now was of
the Red Army, which they were convinced would sooner
or later advance into southern Germany, too.

After the Americans had set up their military government, they did something that made everyone nerv-
ous and upset. Denazification offices were established
and long questionnaires sent to all the households. These
contained questions about the past:

---

*East Prussia, Upper Silesia, Lausitz region: Formerly all parts of Germany;
as a result of the Second World War incorporated into the Soviet Union,
Poland, and East Germany, respectively.

Were you a member of the Nazi party? Since when?

Did you hold a position in the party? If so, which?

Did you play an active role in the party? Yes. No.

Did you in any way support the Nazi government?
Yes. No.

All over the country people were trying to answer these questions.

Political groups gradually began re-forming in the city, the Communists being the first. Among those who joined was a teacher who'd been imprisoned for a long time and without a job even longer. Also signing up were workers who'd sworn allegiance to Ernst Thälmann, the leader of the German Communist party before 1933. This group, calling itself antifascist, wore red insignias, and its members became frequent visitors to the headquarters of the military government. Now and again we would hear about arrests, at first as isolated incidents, then with increasing regularity. Members of the "Anti-FA," as they were called for short, would drive from village to village in a small automobile, picking people up: former mayors, local party leaders, heads of the women's organizations, municipal council members, teachers, and girls who had held positions in the volunteer work corps. We thought some who were picked up deserved to be, but we couldn't figure out why others had been arrested.

One day the automobile drove up to our house. Two men got out and one of them asked, "Is your mother at home? She's supposed to come with us and bring a warm blanket." When he saw that I didn't fully understand, he added, "Yes, *her*. I bet you never expected this!" And out of his pocket he pulled a warrant from the Americans for her arrest.

When I went to mother's office to tell her, I noticed the three poems still hanging on the door. "They've come for you," I said.

For a moment mother was silent, then she burst out laughing. "The Communists," she said. "The Americans relying on the Communists!" Then, putting on her old khaki jacket, she went outside. "There's money in an envelope by the chimney," she told me. "Use it wisely."

While all this was going on, father stood at the door of the house, clutching a small axe. He'll chop them to pieces, I thought. Mother took his hand quietly in hers and said that the matter would soon be cleared up, that they probably just wanted her for questioning. Thunderstruck, we stood there as the car pulled out of the courtyard. "Those bastards," cursed father, and he stalked off toward the woods. He didn't come home until very late that night.

In the evening somebody brought a note from the city. It said that mother had been taken to the district prison with others arrested in the area.

Father paced back and forth in the living room like a caged tiger. "She always had to get involved," he complained. "Always so passionately involved. How often did I beg her to keep her nose out of politics, out of things that were none of her business?"

It was true. Mother had heartily embraced the politics of the Social Democrats, had criticized the German Nationalists and Conservatives, and then had desperately hoped that her fears for the way things were going in Germany were wrong. Yes, she had become involved and had even given lectures organized by the Nazi party. But what hadn't been organized by the party during the last twelve years? Then, when the war started, she had become deeply depressed and had almost cried at the sight of troop trains full of young men waving and singing, "We're setting off, we're setting off for England." In the end she had tried to help the people in the camp, even though reason dictated that she stay as far away from them as possible. To survive difficult times one must be very careful and avoid getting trapped. One mustn't stick one's neck out. Every soldier knows: "Whoever survives is right; whoever runs away is wrong." We had to act according to those principles. And now mother was caught in alien machinery that was supposed to unravel and straighten out something that was deeply ingrained in us Germans. For German feelings had become muddled. Feelings of German greatness, of German honor, of loyalty to the country, of dying for the fatherland — these age-old sentiments had become entangled with something else, the result of which we had witnessed in the valley. It had been such a nice picture we Germans had had of ourselves. Except that a different face had emerged, that of the calculating annihilators of an entire race of people. The fatherland had died for me during the last months of the war,

was a large camp for women and another one for men. Mother was able to smuggle a note out to us. In it she said she was fine and not to worry about her, that she'd be allowed to return home as soon as they had interrogated her.

My brother, who had been discharged from the field hospital, was arrested too. We weren't at all surprised about that as it would have been impossible to explain to any occupying force that the Northern Volunteer Legion of the Waffen-SS had nothing to do with the atrocities that were being reported more and more every day. In the eyes of the German people, many of whom had once considered them the bravest and toughest of soldiers, all members of the Waffen-SS units became outcasts. Those who returned home and were able to escape the searches held by the occupying forces had to face the fear and silent questions of their countrymen: "Where did you serve? Were you one of those . . . ?" If they could, they went into hiding. In prison my brother fell into a diabetic coma, and they called me to come immediately. When I got there, he was lying on a cot, a rolled-up questionnaire stuck in a mug of coffee on the table. He was taken to the hospital and later released.

But mother still did not return.

*F*ather and I tried our best to keep things going. We worked in the fields and the nursery alongside the refugees from the East. On the steps of the house where the girls from Vilika Vovnianka had lived and where Hanne's room had been, there now sat an old granny from the Sudetenland in her wide black skirt with a thick kerchief tied around her head. She wept constantly. With the work-worn hands of a peasant, she wiped the tears from her face, bemoaning her fate.

Father became more and more depressed. I lay awake at night desperately wondering what I could do. Finally, I had an idea. Some of the former camp inmates were still living in Stuttgart and I felt sure they would help. They could bear witness to the fact that mother didn't deserve to be imprisoned. So I took the train to Stuttgart. Part of the city had been evacuated to make room for the former concentration camp inmates who were waiting to emigrate. When I got to this quarter of the city, the streets were filled with hundreds of people, most of them former inmates, milling about and bartering. Among them were some German hucksters and black marketeers — and I felt ashamed to be walking up the street. Eventually I found the house I was looking for and rang the bell. A woman opened the door. She had reddish hair and a thin face that was still quite beautiful despite traces of all that she'd been through.

I introduced myself and she greeted me warmly, for she'd heard about my mother from her husband, who had been one of the doctors in Camp Wiesengrund. I asked if Jakob was there. She knocked on a door and nudged me into a small room containing lots of books and a desk. Jakob slowly rose from the desk and turned around, a puzzled look on his face. I told him what had happened to mother and what I wanted to do. He thought it over and decided that the best course of action would be to draw up a letter addressed to the military government and to get all the former prisoners who were still in Stuttgart to sign it. Jakob said he'd get the signatures and also let me know who the appropriate military authority was.

A few days later he called to say that the letter had been signed. However, he thought it would be better if I delivered it in person to the American headquarters rather than mailing it and he offered to accompany me there.

I met Jakob in the large hall of the Stuttgart railway station, where we were to catch the train to Frankfurt. The station was swarming with American GIs, black marketeers, and lots of German girls wearing spike heels and bright red lipstick. Walking through the hall were German soldiers returning from the prisoner of war camps. Their faces were grim. They glanced neither right nor left but were intent only on getting home. They had defended their fatherland, had escaped from the Russian encirclements or fought all the way back through France. And as Jakob greeted me wearing his high boots and green linen jacket, I suddenly felt oddly out of place.

In the train there were sacks, baskets, and suitcases piled on top of one another and people jamming the corridors. Jakob and I were squeezed in together. While we rode I asked him what his plans were. He said he was waiting for a visa to America. He had been to Poland to look for his sister but had found no trace of her. Poland was like a jungle, he said, with every man for himself and nothing there to eat. Then he started telling me about his past.

He had been up in the mountains with his father when the Germans invaded Poland. They had tried to get back to the town where his mother and sister were, but the German advance had been so swift that they couldn't make it. They were arrested and sent to the ghetto in Warsaw. His father had pleaded with Jakob to escape — alone, without him — so Jakob decided to try it. That was the last time he saw his father. Later he learned he'd been killed in Warsaw. Without papers Jakob was quickly recaptured and sent to a munitions factory as a forced laborer. After that he was taken to Auschwitz, but still being strong and healthy, he was selected for work duty and shipped to Camp Wiesen-grund to work on the construction site.

When Jakob and I arrived in Frankfurt, we went directly to the American headquarters, a tall building with a revolving door. There we saw Americans in uniform walking briskly along the corridors. They didn't look as I had expected them to, wearing battle dress with heavy boots on. They looked more like civilian gentlemen in crisply pressed trousers and street shoes with rubber soles. Speaking in well-modulated voices, mixing German with English, they all carried papers in their hands. The atmosphere was strange, almost eerie.

I waited in the hallway while Jakob went in to speak with an officer. Leaning against the wall, I stared down at my heavy, brown oxfords, which Schauer, the village shoemaker, had made for me — shoes meant for field work, not for the city, but they were the only ones I had.

Jakob came back and reported that we would have to go to the CIC* in Heidelberg. As there was no train to Heidelberg until the following day, we took two rooms at a hotel overnight. It was cold and rainy outside.

I felt I had to see a hairdresser that very day because my hair was starting to grow out and looked awful. I found a shop on the street corner beside the railway station. A girl washed my hair and was combing it out when suddenly she stopped and asked me if I knew I had lice.

*CIC: Counter Intelligence Corps (USA).

"What!" I shrieked.

"Yes, it happens a lot nowadays. I'm not really supposed to work on your hair, but since it's so short, the lice can be combed out."

I could have died of humiliation. Crestfallen, I returned to the hotel.

No sooner had I closed the door to my room, where I'd be able to put my cold feet up on the bed, than there came a knock at the door. Jakob came in. He looked at me in a strange way as we stood facing each other in that dreary, cold hotel room. Suddenly he drew me into his arms and laid his head on my shoulder. "Oh, dear God," he murmured passionately in Polish. An overpowering fist clenched at my heart and I was thrown into complete confusion. What flashed through my mind were the lice in my hair and the girls with the American soldiers — the girls with spiked-heeled shoes and painted lips, the girls who sold themselves for chocolate and cigarettes. "Oh, dear God, *dear God*," I thought too. I asked him to go, please, and he went.

The next morning we took the train to Heidelberg. The city had not been destroyed and was full of American soldiers. While Jakob went into the CIC building to hand in the letter about my mother, I waited outside. Afterwards, we climbed up a path to the old castle that had been burned and pillaged centuries ago and walked through the castle courtyard with its high walls. We stood side by side on the terrace overlooking the old town with its jumble of rooftops and backdrop of tree-covered hills. The sun was setting. The bridges of the

Neckar spread out before us, forming one graceful arch
after another.

I don't know what became of the letter Jakob and I
delivered to the CIC, but mother still didn't return.

Jakob began calling on me. Father noted these visits
with growing concern. One day he took me aside and
said, "I like this fellow a great deal and he's obviously
a man of character, but what you're doing, my *liebes
Kind*, isn't possible."

I knew that myself. I could see how the villagers
turned aside when I wanted to speak to them or how
they suddenly had something urgent to do when I made
my usual stop at the milk depot. One day a neighbor
woman, rake in hand, grabbed me by the sleeve and
said, "I never thought you'd do a thing like that, going
around with a foreigner. And with your mother gone!
And such a strange foreigner, too." I knew what she
really wanted to say, but nobody said such things
anymore.

When Jakob came to visit, we usually went out to the
fields and talked about our lives. He told me about his
grandfather, who had been a wise man — a zaddik,
he called him — and had translated holy texts from
Hebrew. Or we'd stroll up the path beneath the jasmine
bushes through the park to the bee house, where the
once forbidden books still lay hidden behind the honey-
combs. We would climb the Silla Hopp and, standing
together by the little gate where Stephan and his friends
had wanted to hang lanterns for my wedding day, we'd
watch the silver moon rise over the dark outline of the

hills. But I couldn't get out of my mind an old nursery rhyme that our nanny had taught me as a child:

> There were two royal children
> In love with one another.
> The water lay so deep between
> They could not reach each other.

Jakob was usually in good spirits even though he had no plans for the future except to go to America. Patiently and gallantly he pleaded with me to come with him, but America seemed like such a strange and distant country. We were still struggling to find a bridge across the abyss fate had placed between us.

On Sunday afternoons I used to go to Stuttgart to visit Jakob and his friends. When I returned home in the evening, I would stand at the window dreaming of him. He was different from other young people I'd known — so solid and imperturbable that nothing, not even the cruelest circumstances, seemed to set him off course. He was of the stuff of prophets, the great prophets the Bible tells us about. But how strong was *I*? Could I leave the fields behind or the wind blowing through the green wheat? Could I leave the smells of autumn, the leaves under the trees in the park and the odor of the newly pressed wine? Could I leave the old vineyard where father used to paint or the little church tower whose bells signaled a pause in the day's labors? Could the trust that Jakob and I now shared endure after all that had been done to his people by mine? Finding no answer, I would go out into the night and sit in the park beneath the high birch trees, praying to the Holy Virgin Mary to have mercy on me and show me the way.

My old world lay shattered, and I could not seem to find the courage to grasp a new one.

We regularly received notes from mother that had been smuggled out of the camp. The notes always said the same thing, that she was well and would be home soon. Mother had been away for almost six months when one day she wandered into the courtyard wearing her old khaki jacket and carrying the same blanket under her arm. She had gained weight and looked cheerful. The Americans had dismissed her from the huge camp without an interrogation or a trial; in fact, no one had bothered about her at all. She had not even heard of the letter signed by the former inmates of Camp Wiesengrund until we told her about it.

Mother related many stories about the American camp and the thousands of women from every walk of life locked up there. Although I listened to her stories, they didn't really reach me. I was completely preoccupied with my own problems, for Jakob's visits had become less and less frequent and finally had stopped altogether.

One day when I was working out in the nursery, three Americans from the radio station in Stuttgart came to see me. They wanted me to give a radio talk about Camp Wiesengrund. "You've seen it. Describe it as it was. There is so much disbelief among the populace here."

I had seen it all right. I had only to close my eyes to

relive all those scenes I had witnessed. I would carry
them with me until the end of my days.

But now all the German refugees were pouring in
from the East. By the millions they came, wave upon
never-ending wave of them entering the British and
American occupied zones. The tales of their flight were
terrible. We heard how streams of men, women, and
children, pulling sleds and dragging suitcases, had been
pursued by Red Army tanks. How when the tanks caught
up with the refugees, they crushed them into the snow
under their giant treads and then turned around until
the bodies were ground to scraps. How whenever Russian soldiers found women, they raped them, and how
afterwards many of the victims had killed themselves.

What the Allies had discovered when they pushed
back the German army and advanced into our country
— fifty boxcars filled with corpses on the tracks in Dachau, the horrors of Auschwitz and Maidanek, of Bergen-Belsen and Buchenwald and dozens upon dozens
of camps like Wiesengrund — all these horrors were
widely reported in the press with pictures. The occupation forces couldn't understand why so many Germans simply refused to believe these reports. But few
had known the truth about the camps and fewer still
had witnessed one as I had. Having endured the war,
the destruction of their cities, flight from the Russians,
hunger, and loss of homeland, they couldn't take in yet
another dimension of suffering too enormous to be
grasped. Also, so much propaganda had been poured
over their heads during the last twelve years that these

reports were often considered to be just one more round of horror propaganda — only this time from the other side.

No, I told the American officers, I didn't want to talk about Wiesengrund. It wouldn't be of any use now. They left the nursery disappointed.

Later that year, the French set up a military tribunal in Rastatt to handle the cases of those guards from Camp Wiesengrund who had been captured and imprisoned. They summoned mother as a witness. With tears in her eyes she told us what had happened that day. There in the dock sat the commandant; SS leaders Hecker, Pill, and Sommer; and Dischmann, the camp doctor. Möller was also led in, blind now as the result of an illness. Dr. Poulsen, who had been summoned from Norway to testify, told the court, "I will never be able to put out of my mind the pictures of human misery that I saw during my captivity in this camp."

When mother stepped up to the witness stand, the judges all rose and the presiding judge said, "You are one German who helped to save civilization. You have acted honorably and with charity. The court wishes to thank you for that today. . . . "

I only saw Jakob once more. I had been accepted at the university to study agriculture. My classmates there had all been in the army, some for six or seven years. Their experiences had been so different from mine that I felt like a stranger among them. Some had been with the troops that had advanced all through Europe and into Africa and Russia. Others had just entered the army when the retreat began. They had been put in prisoner of war camps or, if wounded, had recovered in hospitals. Some of them had originally come from Danzig or Silesia, Pomerania or East Prussia — homelands they could not return to.

The conviction was widespread among these students that sooner or later the Russians would mount an attack against the western part of Germany. All day long discussions went on about what they'd do if that happened. "Sure we'd try to fight," they said, "if we could get hold of rifles." But to order other men to fight — that they swore they would never do again.

Then one day I received a brief note from Jakob saying he wanted to talk to me. It was late afternoon when we met at the streetcar stop near the main building of the university. He was wearing his high boots and an open shirt, his green jacket slung over his shoulder. We walked through the botanical garden down a narrow path lined with low boxwood hedges. "I'll be leaving for America in a few days," he said. "Are you coming with me?" He asked this question gallantly, even though we both knew it was too late for us. As if from a distance, I heard myself say, "No, I can't."

We walked on in silence. There was a harmony between us — of footfall and of sadness. Maybe we had been meant for each other, but we'd been born in the wrong place, of the wrong parents, and definitely at the wrong time.

The early evening sky was bathed in purple as we turned back to the waiting streetcar. Its interior was brightly lit up. Jakob mounted the steps and stood in the aisle, hanging on to the strap with both hands. His head inclined, he looked down at me with his large, dark eyes. Like Jesus crucified, I thought. Then the streetcar slowly pulled away and turned the corner.